PERSONAL NARRATIVE OF A JOURNEY FROM INDIA TO ENGLAND

PERSONAL NARRATIVE OF A JOURNEY FROM INDIA TO ENGLAND,

BY BUSSORAH, BAGDAD, THE RUINS OF BABYLON, CURDISTAN, THE COURT OF PERSIA, THE WESTERN SHORE OF THE CASPIAN SEA, ASTRAKHAN, NISHNEY NOVOGOROD, MOSCOW, AND ST. PETERSBURGH, IN THE YEAR 1824

By

CAPTAIN, THE HON. GEORGE KEPPEL

SECOND EDITION

IN TWO VOLUMES
VOL. II

Published by

Gyan Publishing House
5, Ansari Road
Daryaganj, New Delhi-110002
Phone: 011-47034999, 9811692060
E-mail: books@gyanbooks.com

Distribution Network
gyanbooks.com
India, USA, Canada, UK, Australia, France

ISBN : 978-81-212-6452-5 (Set)
978-81-212-6450-1 (PB)
First Published, 1827

2nd Impression 2022

Printed at: Gyan Press, Delhi.

PERSONAL NARRATIVE OF A JOURNEY FROM INDIA TO ENGLAND (VOL. II)

Author: CAPTAIN, THE HON. GEORGE KEPPEL

From an oriental Drawing — *Pr.td by Engelmann & Co*

A LESGUY TARTAR

Publis.d by H.y Colburn London Dec 1. 1826.

PERSONAL NARRATIVE

OF A

JOURNEY FROM

INDIA TO ENGLAND,

BY BUSSORAH, BAGDAD, THE RUINS OF BABYLON,

CURDISTAN, THE COURT OF PERSIA,

THE WESTERN SHORE OF THE CASPIAN SEA, ASTRAKHAN,

NISHNEY NOVOGOROD, MOSCOW, AND ST. PETERSBURGH,

IN THE YEAR 1824.

BY

CAPTAIN, THE HON. GEORGE KEPPEL.

SECOND EDITION.

IN TWO VOLUMES.

VOL. II.

1827.

CONTENTS

OF THE SECOND VOLUME.

CHAPTER I.

CHAPTER II.

CHAPTER III.

CHAPTER IV.

CHAPTER V.

CHAPTER VI.

CHAPTER VII.

CHAPTER VIII.

CHAPTER IX.

CHAPTER X.

CHAPTER XI.

NARRATIVE,

&c. &c.

CHAPTER I.

An Illyaut Breakfast—Beautiful Female—One of the King's Wives—Town of Harounabad—Beauty of the Women—Mahidesht—Escorted into Kermanshah—Description of the Town—An Order of Knighthood—Character of Mohumud Ali Meerza, the late Prince of Kermanshah—Anecdote of His Highness and Gaspar Khan—Visit from the Prince of Kermanshah.

April 20.—Our scolding yesterday had due effect with the muleteer, and we got away very expeditiously. We commenced our march at the rising of the moon, by which our movements were regulated. The road was in general good, though in some parts exceedingly stony. We continued ascending till day-break, when we reached a small plain.

As the sun rose, it reflected its rays on a scene as beautiful as it was varied. On one side was a succession of thickly-wooded hills, exhibiting an almost endless variety of foliage; on the other an extensive plain, at the base of rude and craggy mountains, covered with the brightest verdure, the uniformity of which was relieved by the numerous black encampments of the Coordish wanderers, and by the occasional patches of cultivation observable in the immediate neighbourhood of their tents. The lofty Elwund, raising its snowy head, seemed to peer in towering majesty over the surrounding landscape, and formed a beautiful background to the scene; while a numerous caravan, tracing its way through the mazy windings of the road, added not a little to the living part of the picture.

The chief person of the caravan was adjusting his dress by a small looking-glass, and rode up to us with it in his hand. After the usual salutations, he enquired whence we came and what were our names, which he noted down in a memorandum-book. The caravan consisted of a number of families, apparently of good condition. Among them were some females, all closely veiled, riding in couples in covered baskets, with the exception of some few who rode astride on mules.

Since entering the Persian dominions we have been much struck with the marked civility of all ranks of people, who have always saluted us in passing. We passed numerous Illyaut encampments, scattered over the valley in every direction.

On this march we observed a number of carcase-shells, and broken gun-carriages, &c.

Pursuing our journey, we were addressed by some Illyauts, who, pointing to their tents, situate at some little distance, in the ascent of the mountains, invited us to breakfast with them. Messrs. Lamb and Hart, being much oppressed by the heat, declined the invitation; but Mr. Hamilton and myself, relying on their proverbial reverence for the rites of hospitality, went with them to their tents, taking with us only two servants.

The tents of these Coords were ranged in one long street, and disposed as booths at a fair: there appeared to be abundance of cattle, but arranged in no kind of order; horses, cows, and sheep, being indiscriminately mixed with men, women, and children. We were shown into a spacious tent. A carpet was spread for us, on a raised platform about three feet high, where, after taking off our capacious red travelling-boots, we were desired to seat ourselves in the manner most convenient. A breakfast of warm milk, eggs, and bread, was placed before us; and the whole camp turned out to see the Ferunghees at their meal, which, to amuse them, we ate in the English fashion.

Delighted as all around us appeared to be with the novelty of our costume, we were not less gratified than they, in beholding the varied group of heads, forming an amphitheatre in front of us; the children standing in the foreground, behind them the women, and, towering over all, the bearded faces of the men, exhibiting a collection of countenances lighted up with a variety of expression, in which curiosity was predominant.

Our hosts talked much of the excellent sporting the mountains afforded. I asked them if they busied themselves much in cultivating the land; to which they replied, that they only tilled just sufficient for their own immediate wants. Mr. Hamilton's servant, Mohumud Ali, who never lost an opportunity of becoming the spokesman, finished the sentence by saying, "What do they care for cultivation, when their principal trade is robbery?" a remark to which the Coords smilingly nodded assent.

Our attention to the general group was suddenly arrested by the appearance of a young female, about seventeen years of age, whom we thought the most beautiful woman we had ever seen. She was leaning against the pole of the tent, with her head supported by her left arm, and was gazing at us with the most fixed attention: her jet black hair flowed about her in unconfined luxuriance; the brilliancy of her eyes, heightened by the dark stain of the *surmeh*, seemed riveted with a curiosity not the less gratifying to us from knowing that we excited it; her half-closed mouth displayed teeth of the most regular form and perfect whiteness. Her person, almost entirely exposed by the opening of her loose shirt, (the only covering she wore,) displayed a form of the most perfect symmetry: no sculptor could do justice to such a model.

We reached Harounabad in half an hour's ride, crossed a small bridge, and found our tents ready pitched on the opposite side, near the bank of a rapid stream.

We were advised most strongly by the inhabitants of the town to lodge in the caravanserai, on account of the numerous hordes of Illyauts, who, they said, would be likely to attack us in the night. As we were more in dread of vermin than of robbers, we said that we preferred remaining where we were, as we were well able to protect ourselves—a boast we thought it necessary frequently to repeat, thinking our safety depended considerably on confirming these banditti in the high notions we knew they entertained of European prowess.

In the course of the morning, one of the

khanums, wives of the King of Persia, encamped close to us: she had just arrived from Tabriz, the court of Abbas Meerza, the Prince Royal of Persia, and was proceeding to Kerbela on a pilgrimage. She had only three small tents; her establishment, though inferior to ours, was sufficiently large for one of fifteen hundred partakers of the royal bed. As the lady belonged to the court of the Prince Royal of Persia, who has always been very attentive to our countrymen, we sent to inform her that we were going to Tabriz, and should be happy to execute any commission with which she might honour us. This message produced a visit from two of the principal persons with her; and shortly after, her confidential eunuch came to thank us for our civility. He was a handsome young man of about two and twenty, very lively, and remarkably courteous in his manners; he stayed for about a quarter of an hour; and spoke in very high terms of our countrymen at Tabriz, particularly Dr. Cormick, the prince's physician, who is deservedly a favourite, not only with the Persians, but with all who have the pleasure of his acquaintance. The eunuch spoke also with much friendship of our late shipmate, Futteh Ali Khan, who, to have merited the encomiums bestowed on him, must have behaved much better at Tabriz as the dependant of a prince, than in India, when a prince himself.

Before dusk, we strolled into the town, and, as usual, collected a crowd about us: we were by this time so accustomed to the gaze of the inhabitants, that we rather courted communication than otherwise, with a view to lose no opportunity of becoming acquainted with the disposition and habits of the people. We found them very civil, and instead of objecting to our visit, they seemed much pleased with us for observing them. The women were without veils, and for the most part occupied in making those beautiful carpets, for which this country is so celebrated. Many of these were offered us as presents; a mode adopted in the East for disposing of goods for double their value, inasmuch as those who tender the gift expect a sum in return, correspondent to the consequence they are pleased to assign the party to whom they make the offering.

Harounabad is built on a gradual slope; the houses are very low, with flat connecting roofs, in successive lines one above the other: as the backs are level with the ground, the principal communication is in many places along the roofs, and we were frequently surprised in finding ourselves walking on the tops of inhabited dwellings, when we thought we were traversing the solid ground.

This town, as its name implies, was formerly a residence of the famous Caliph Haroun, but we could not trace any remains of a palace fit to receive so magnificent a monarch. The town is small, and may contain about a thousand souls. It is remarkable for the beauty of its women, probably on account of the nearly perpetual Spring of the climate. To judge from some we saw washing clothes in the river, the fame of this place has not been ill bestowed. Independent, therefore, of the temperature of Harounabad, the luxuriant beauty of the women might have induced so gay a monarch to take up his occasional abode in this mountainous retreat.

April 21.—We left Harounabad at three in the morning; and continued ascending, for the first four hours, a circuitous road: we afterwards passed through two deep basins formed by the surrounding mountains, having a considerable descent to the East. At ten o'clock we reached Mahidesht, situate in an extensive plain of an oval form, with numerous small villages scattered over it. The snow was still lying on the surrounding hills.

Notwithstanding our dislike to a caravanserai, we were obliged to take up our quarters there, as well on account of the robbers, who were said to be very numerous, as that there was no encamping ground in the vicinity. We established ourselves over the gateway, the post of honour in these buildings. By this arrangement we were more commodiously accommodated, and avoided the necessity of coming in contact with the numerous badly embalmed corpses, with which the other parts of the caravanserai were promiscuously strewed.

As we were only one stage from Kermanshah, we sent forward by a servant the letters with which we had been entrusted: one was from Aga Saikeis to Meerza Ahedy, the minister of war to the prince; and the others from the Chief of artillery to Messieurs Court and De Veaux, two French officers in the service of his Highness. With the recollection of the inconveniences attendant on the hospitality of the British agent, we sent to beg that we might either be allowed to occupy a vacant house, or to pitch our tents in any of the gardens adjoining the town.

April 22.—At three this morning we started for Kermanshah, distant from the caravanserai fourteen miles. The plain of Mahidesht is ten miles in breadth, four of which we traversed yesterday, and the remaining six this morning. Thence, after ascending for a little way, we went through a small valley between two mountains. The remainder of the road led over a succession of low hills. The morning was very fine. In rounding a mountain, we came somewhat suddenly in sight of the smiling and fruitful valley of Kermanshah ; a numerous caravan of pilgrims passed us, on its road to Kerbela.

Three miles from the town, as we were descending a hill, we saw marshalled at a short distance a gay party on horseback, equipped in the Persian dress. As soon as we came in sight, they met us at full speed: as they approached, two of the party galloped forward and threw the jereed. It was easy to perceive that this gaily caparisoned cavalcade had assembled in compliment to us. We were for a moment in doubt who they were; for we looked in vain for the European costume: our conjectures were soon set at rest by one of the company, with a long beard, saluting us in the European military fashion, and in the French language, bidding us welcome to Kermanshah. The party consisted of the European residents of the city, together with their united trains of servants and followers: of these there were Messieurs De Veaux and Court, the two French officers, to whom we had letters; two Italians; and another person, calling himself a Spaniard, of whom more hereafter.

We did not come within sight of the town till we had entered a deep and broad ravine, at the top of which it is situated. Kermanshah is encompassed with gardens, and decked with numerous small kiosks (pleasure-houses). It is laid out in walks, canals, and reservoirs of water, all of which have a picturesque effect on the approach. The Kurasou, a river, or rather a mountain torrent, runs through the centre of the town: the overflowing of its banks, which occasionally happens, is attended with very serious injury. Three years ago an event of this description occurred, in which the lower parts of the town and a considerable portion of the inhabitants were entirely swept away. We were conducted by Messieurs Court and De Veaux to their house, and pressed so much to remain there during our stay, that we could not help yielding to their solicitations, though opposed to the resolution we had formed of not becoming the guests of any one. Soon after our arrival, Hassan Khan, the governor, came on the part of the Prince to tell us that a house had been prepared for our reception, and that his Highness desired we would consider ourselves as his guests; an invitation we declined, with due acknowledgments for the Prince's hospitality and condescension.

We passed the remainder of the morning in conversation with our new acquaintances, who related many interesting particulars of the late war with the Pasha of Bagdad, in which they appear to have borne a very conspicuous part. These gentlemen and the Spanish officer, Senor Oms, are all *khans* (lords) of Persia, and knights of the lion and sun, as well as of another order, the insignia of which are a star, with the curious device of two lions fighting for the Persian crown. This order was instituted by the king's eldest son, Mohumud Ali Meerza (the late prince governor of this country), and derives its origin from the following circumstance :—

Some years since, the present King, in conformity to one of the most ancient laws of Persia,* assembled his sons for the purpose of nominating a successor to the throne, on the event of his death. Abbas Meerza, the king's second son, was promised this high dignity. All the princes present bowed in obedience to the declaration of the royal will, with the exception of Mohumud Ali Meerza, who alone stood erect. Unawed by the presence of his father and sovereign, he refused to acknowledge the decree. His resistance to the royal mandate was conveyed in the

* In the same manner Cyrus, previous to his expedition against the Massagetæ, appointed Cambyses his successor to the Persian throne.

following bold and energetic language: "May God preserve the King of Kings; but if my brother and myself should have the misfortune to survive your Majesty," (and he half unsheathed his sword as he finished the sentence,) "*this* shall decide the accession to the throne." The two warlike brothers nodded mutual defiance, and were, up to the period of Mohumud Ali's death, open and avowed enemies.

On the return of the French officers from some successful expedition against the Turks, they asked the Prince to institute some order of knighthood as a reward for their services. Mohumud Ali acceded; and not forgetting his oath of enmity to his brother, founded an order having the appropriate device of two lions fighting for the crown, in allusion to the circumstance related. It is remarkable that these insignia of opposition to the despotic will of the sovereign were openly sanctioned by the King himself; while Mohumud Ali, heretofore ignorant of the value attached to ribands in Europe, was surprised and gratified to find that his European auxiliaries were content with so cheap a remuneration for their many and important services.

Mohumud Ali is generally considered to have been the most warlike prince of the present (kajar) dynasty. His memory is held in the highest veneration by the tribes over whom he ruled. A man who could lead his followers to conquest and plunder must have been acceptable to these wild mountaineers, who had inherited a thirst for rapine from a long line of predatory ancestors. The French officers too are equally enthusiastic with the Coords in praise of their late commander; his daring spirit appearing to have found a congenial feeling in men whose love of military adventure has made war the highest enjoyment of life. In 1814, when the reverses of Napoleon appeared to have completely closed the prospects of a soldier in Europe, they sought and found in the troubled regions of the East an ample field for the gratification of their darling passion.

As mention has been incidentally made of the pursuits of these officers, it may not be amiss to state a fact, perhaps not generally known, that a number of military men, of different nations of Europe, are at this moment wandering over Asia, offering their services to the Asiatic princes. Seven or eight European officers were at one time employed in this remote province (Kermanshah), the greater part of whom are now dispersed over the East. To what point they have shaped their course, Messrs. Court and De Veaux could give us no account, though of themselves, their past history, and their future prospects, they scrupled not to talk in the most unreserved manner. They had at one time, they said, intended to have gone up the Indus, for the purpose of offering their services to an Indian prince, who, they understood, wanted European officers to conduct his forces against the English; but they had been induced to abandon their design on hearing of the great impediments likely to be thrown in their way by our Indian government.

Among other anecdotes, our hosts related one respecting the late prince and our Bagdad acquaintance Gaspar Khan, which may be worth inserting, as it serves to illustrate a mode of punishment common at Kermanshah—of burying a man alive, with his head downwards and his legs in the air.

A short time ago, Gaspar Khan, who is employed by the King in commercial transactions, was passing from the court of Persia through Kermanshah, where he was received with much civility by Mohumud Ali Meerza, who took him round one of his gardens. In the course of the walk, his

Highness asked Gaspar, if the garden was not deficient in something. The Khan, as in duty bound, replied, that the garden was quite perfect, and required no addition. Mohumud Ali replied, "Yes, there is a tree that I have long wanted: it is called Gaspar Khan, and it shall be planted immediately." Then changing his tone, he said, "You have been prejudicing the King's mind against me, so prepare for instant death." The Khan begged hard for life, which the fear of ill treating a king's agent most probably induced him to grant.

At 12 o'clock, the Persian hour of morning repast, we were summoned to a plentiful meal, combining a happy mixture of European and Asiatic cookery. We had neither chairs nor tables, the cloth being spread on the floor, and we seated in the oriental fashion. Our distress in this uneasy posture presented a singularly striking contrast to the obvious comfort enjoyed by our hosts, to whose muscles habit had given a flexibility certainly unknown to ours. The feast was seasoned by some excellent wine, made from the fine grapes of the neighbourhood, which was cooled by frozen snow brought from the mountain, the silver summit of which was visible from the apartment. A long abstinence from wine had made us more than usually subject to the powerful influence of the generous beverage; and after a few quickly repeated bumpers, our heads felt the effect of the potations so strongly, as to suggest the advantage, if not the absolute necessity, of taking a siesta.

April 23.—We went this morning to pay our respects to Mohumud Hosein Meerza, the prince governor. His Highness seemed disposed to treat us with more than ordinary civility; for he told the French officers that he should allow us to be seated in his presence, and, as this is an honour never granted to any of his court, he would advise them not to be present at the interview. These preliminaries settled, we set out in full uniform to the palace, where we found Hassan Khan, the governor, in waiting to conduct us to the Prince. We passed, in our way to the hall of audience, through a number of passages, not remarkable for cleanliness, and arrived at an oblong court, in the centre of which a fountain played. At the top of this court, the Prince was seated near an open window. At stated intervals, the Governor made profound obeisances; but as every thing military is in vogue in this country, we saluted his Highness merely by putting our hands to our hats. In conformity to Persian etiquette, he took no notice of the compliment, and even seemed to be unconscious of our presence. On our nearer approach, he bade us welcome; so leaving our slippers in the court, we entered the hall; and, following the directions of the Governor, seated ourselves near the doorway.

A few minutes before our interview, Monsieur De Veaux had been with the Prince, to receive his instructions relative to the issue of some clothing to those troops who were to escort the body of his father to Meshed Ali; and also, respecting some other matters connected with the order of the funeral from Kermanshah, a ceremony which was to take place in two days. As the inspection of these arrangements was made in the public square, the Prince thought it necessary to play the mourner on the occasion. No sooner did he come in sight of the coffin which contained the remains of his father, than he threw off his cap, covered his head with ashes, and, rolling himself on the ground, bitterly bewailed the loss of so illustrious a prince and so good a father. Having performed this ceremonial of grief with all the usual Eastern decorum, he re-adjusted his cap, clothed himself in a scarlet robe, and in the short interval between the inspection and our visit, laid down the part of the mourner, and re-assumed that of the prince, so speedily indeed, that if we had not had a peep behind the curtain, we could not have believed that one actor could so speedily have performed two such different parts.

His Highness, hearing I spoke Persian, put a number of questions, with such a rapidity that I often felt puzzled to give suitable answers. His first interrogatories were, why we had not accepted his hospitality, and whether we were satisfied with the Governor, at the same time casting an inquisitive glance at that personage. By a prompt answer in the affirmative, I in all probability saved the soles of the Governor's feet from the bastinado, a cheap compliment, and, though at the expense of as high a functionary, not unusually conferred on a guest whom an Eastern prince "delighteth to honour." Having enquired our respective ages, he wished to know the numbers of our wives and children; but when he found we were totally unprovided in both these necessaries of life, he urged us all to marry the moment we returned to Europe. As he repeated this injunction often, I thought to escape from the oppressiveness of his reiterated advice by briefly observing, that in our country we were deemed too young to enter on so serious a state as matrimony. I could not have stumbled on a more inappropriate excuse. His Highness immediately informed us, that though younger by three years than either Mr. Hart or myself, he had been married some years, and, as I afterwards heard, had eighteen wives, a proportionate number of children, and was daily adding to both these branches of his establishment. The last, though, in his opinion, not the least important observation of this sapient Prince, was directed to the scantiness of hair which our faces exhibited, each of us having only mustaches, which are indispensable in this country; but this scanty allowance not corresponding with his idea of the toilette, he strongly urged our wearing long beards, at the same time, with much complacency, stroking his own, which, for a youth of two and twenty, was of most precocious growth. I endeavoured to apologize for our want of whiskers by observing, that it was not the fashion of our country; though I should have been scarcely justified in urging such a plea, had I seen the present "men about town," whose hairy cheeks would almost excite the envy of the great Shah himself.

CHAPTER II.

Three Arab Visitors—A Chieftain—An Astrologer—A Moolah—Ancient Sculptures at Tauk Bostaun—Chosroes, Shereen, and Furhaud—Persian Dance—Equestrian Evolutions—Turcoman breed of Horses—Persian mode of clearing the way for a great Man—Funeral Procession of Mohumud Ali Meerza—The Moolahi Báshee—Suleiman Khan Kuruzungeer, and the Sect of Illahi.

On returning to our quarters, we found Messieurs Court and De Veaux seated in the garden, in company with three Arabs, all of whom had lately fled for protection from the present Pasha of Bagdad.

One of these was the young Arab Chieftain, to whom we were indebted for our information respecting the Calor banditti. This young man's father had, a few months back, with only forty men, defended a fortress against Davoud Pasha, but had ultimately been induced to surrender, on a solemn assurance of protection. In the interview that followed the capitulation, the Pasha, unmindful of his promise, caused his head to be struck off, and packed up in a parcel, as a present to the Grand Signior, to adorn one of the spikes at Constantinople.

The second victim of oppression, in some measure, deserved his fate. He was, by profession, an astrologer, and might have pursued his divinations undisturbed, had he not interfered in the domestic concerns of Davoud Pasha, a man little likely to allow such conduct to pass with impunity. It appears that one of the Pasha's wives, who had for a time held a considerable sway over his affections, was obliged to resign it in favour of some more youthful beauty. The discarded lady, in a fit of jealousy, applied to this dealer in occult sciences to exert his supernatural influence, either in alienating the affection of Davoud from her rival, or in sowing dissension amongst the whole establishment, in revenge for her neglected charms. Whether by magic influence or not, certain it is, he so far succeeded in the latter request, that he set the whole haram in an uproar. The Pasha, on discovering the destroyer of his peace, immediately issued orders for his apprehension. A timely flight saved the head of the Magician, though he left behind him property to the amount of ten thousand piasters, which has, in all probability, consoled the Pasha in his domestic afflictions.

The third person in this group had no claims whatever on our commiseration. His name was Moolah Ali, an Arab, though he wore the Persian dress; one with whom murder and every other crime had long been familiar. There was nothing, however, in his appearance to justify this supposition, nor in his features could there be distinguished any of those marks with which our romance-writers are wont to stamp the countenance of a murderer. On the contrary, his mild eye beamed with intelligence when he spoke, and his mouth was lighted up with so pleasing a smile, that the diabolical matter of his speech was often lost in attending to the pleasing manner of his delivery. Like many an Asiatic I have seen, his countenance was so entirely at variance with his conduct, as to set at nought all the boasted science of a physiognomist; his manners were remarkably captivating, and possessed that easy polish for which the natives of these countries are so remarkable. His conscience never troubled him with "air-drawn daggers;" he had a real one in his girdle, to be used as inclination prompted.

Not many weeks before we saw this Moolah, he was one of the principal persons of Mendali, a Turkish town near the frontier. In those days he was the bosom friend of Davoud Pasha, "his best of cut-throats" and most willing instrument of assassination. It was during his intimacy with the Pasha that, on the day of some religious festival, he invited sixteen persons to a feast, and placing a confidential agent between each guest, caused every one of them to be put to death, himself giving the signal of slaughter by plunging a dagger into the breast of the person beside him. Such feats as these we may find in the histories of savage countries. Among all barbarians, the virtue of hospitality, so vaunted, has rarely, if ever, withstood the excitement of revenge or avarice.

It is natural to suppose, that a friendship between two such persons as the Moolah and the Pasha, cemented as it was by guilt, could not be of long duration; accordingly we soon find these brethren in iniquity the most deadly foes; each beginning to exercise on the kindred, what he could not effect on the head of the family. Seventy of the Moolah's relations have fallen victims to the revenge of the Pasha; his father is chained in a prison in Bagdad, and ten thousand piasters are set upon his own head. In the mean time, he has not been backward in retaliation. Leaving the town of Mendali, attended by several of his tribe, he sallied forth into the Desert, attacked the Turkish caravans, and (to use his own expression) struck off, at every opportunity, the heads of all those wearing turbans.* The women of the party fell victims to the licentious passions of himself and followers, and other brutal excesses were committed by these ruffians, that would scarcely be credited in our own country.

Observing us listen with much interest to

* The turban distinguishes the Turks from the Persians, who wear sheepskin caps.

this detail of crime, and taking for granted that our attention was a mark of sympathy, he said, with an air of gratitude, "How kind it is of you to enter so warmly into my pursuits!"

During our stay at Kermanshah we were in daily intercourse with this accomplished villain, who upon most subjects possessed a degree of information far beyond the generality of his countrymen. Of his deeds and projects he always spoke with the most unblushing effrontery, telling us that his schemes of plunder were only suspended till the remains of Mohumud Ali Meerza should be safely deposited in the holy burying-ground. Any act of hostility committed by him while a retainer of the court, would probably be retaliated by some insult to the corpse; and this would make the Prince his enemy, with whom it was so much his interest to keep on good terms; "but," added he, "that business once settled, Allah grant that the Pasha may fall into my hands, and then I will tear out his heart and drink his blood." On our first salutation in a morning he would always repeat the words, "Inshallah Pasha," (God willing, the Pasha,) supplying the rest of the sentence by significantly passing his finger across his throat.*

We one day asked the Moolah how he generally deprived his enemies of life? "That," replied he, "is as I can catch them. Some I have killed in battle, others I have stabbed sleeping." Another time we had the curiosity to examine his pistols, which, we had often remarked, were studded with several red nails. On enquiring the reason, he told us that each nail was to commemorate the death of some enemy who had fallen by that weapon.

April 25.—We went this morning to examine the celebrated ancient sculptures in this

* In allusion to the Turkish form of passing a sentence of death on a criminal.

neighbourhood, at a place called Tauk Bostaun, distant six miles from the town. We paid another visit to these antiquities the day before our departure from Kermanshah. They are situated in two recesses, excavated in the west side of the mountain, the principal of which is twenty-four feet seven inches wide, and twenty feet four inches deep. The entrance is a handsome semicircular arch, ornamented with well-executed sculpture. The pillars to the spring of the arch have elegant flower ornaments in pannels. Above these, on each side, are winged female figures, in Grecian drapery, holding in their right hands, which are stretched towards each other, circular fillets of jewels, and in their left, bowls of an Etruscan shape, apparently containing wreaths of flowers, similar to what are used in India on occasions of ceremony. These figures are dressed in loose flowing robes, with jackets fitting close to the body, distinctly displaying the upper part of the shape: round the waist of the entire figure is a band, fastened with a clasp of jewels. The features appeared to be Abyssinian; the hair is in regular curls on each side of the face. Between these figures, on the top of the arch, is a winged crescent; the sides of the recess are wholly covered with sculptures. Facing the entrance is a colossal figure on horseback, in such high relief, that only the left shoulder of the horse and horseman adhere to the rock. This is said to be Rustam, the most celebrated hero of Persian romance. He is clad in chain armour, similar to that worn by English warriors in the early times of the Crusades, and by the Coords of the present day. He carries in the right hand a poised spear; in the left, a circular shield; and a quiver of arrows are bound on the right thigh. The horse is richly caparisoned, after the manner common in India at this time. The right hand of Rustam is broken, as are part of the head, and the off hind-leg of the horse.

Immediately above the statue are three figures, dressed in rich robes, said to be King Khosro, or Chosroes, with his wife, Shereen, on his right, and her lover, Furhaud, on his left hand. Both these last have circular wreaths in their right hands, which they are holding up to Chosroes, whose right hand is stretched to receive them from Furhaud, and whose left rests on a large double-handed sword. On the head costume of Chosroes is a sort of ball, observable on the coins of the Sassanian kings. Shereen appears to be holding an Etruscan pitcher, from which a fluid is issuing, apparently in the act of libation. This is thought to have some allusion to the neighbouring stream. The faces of these figures were mutilated by order of Nadir Shah, who wished to destroy the whole group. On each side of the recess, are two fluted pillars with flowered capitals, somewhat resembling the Corinthian order. On the right side of the recess is the representation of a boar-hunt with elephants, in which are several hundred figures of men, women, and animals. This side exhibits the appearance of a large jungle full of game. In the centre is a lake, on the surface of which are observed swans and four boats. In the two largest boats are two figures of a size superior to the others, and armed with a bow, an eastern mark of sovereignty. The two monarchs are attended with a band of female harpers. The boats are of a peculiar construction, dissimilar to any I have seen in these countries, but propelled, after the ancient as well as modern manner, by two men, one at the prow, and the other at the stern. Two sides of the jungle are lined with men on elephants, which animals (as is common in Indian boar-hunting) appear to be driving them towards the sportsmen, who with their bows and arrows seem to do considerable execution. A small portion towards the corner is appropriated to those men and elephants disposing of the dead game

The human figures here are in the Grecian costume. On the opposite side to this group is a deer-hunt, which evidently was never finished. In this portion there are three royal personages mounted on horseback, all armed with bows; but one appears of superior rank to the others, as he has a parasol held over his head. On the top, at this side, is a band of musicians playing on various instruments, amongst which may be recognized the tam-tam, the trumpet, the harp, and the flute.

I cannot close the description of this beautiful specimen of ancient workmanship without giving a short account of a more modern production of the chisel, which was intended to eclipse the ancient sculpture.

Above the boar-hunt, executed in very high relief, are three figures of colossal stature, but executed with true Persian disregard to symmetry or proportion. They are intended to represent the late Prince Mohumud Ali Meerza, his son the present Governor of Kermanshah, and the Khojahi Bashee (chief of the eunuchs), to whom the arts are indebted for this superlative piece of barbarous sculpture.

The figures are clothed in the full costume of the Persian court, the princes wearing their royal tiaras, and the chief of the eunuchs himself, in his dress of state, standing by in attendance. This personage, being of opinion that the mere stone gave too faint a delineation of real life, resolved to press into the service of statuary, her sister Painting. The sculpture is daubed and gilded in such a manner, as to eclipse, in the opinion of the natives, the more unpretending performance of the ancients.

A short distance to the left of this excavation is situated the second. In it are two figures holding in their hands a circular wreath: a figure stands behind that on the right with a bâton in his hand, and is urging or enforcing some counsel. The two figures appear to be cementing a treaty of peace over the body of a fallen enemy. On each side of the figures is an inscription in the ancient Persic language, which has been translated by M. de Sacy to the following effect: "This is the figure of the adorer of Ormusd, the excellent Shapoor, King of Kings of Iran and Aniran, sprung from the celestial race of Gods, son of the adorer of Ormusd, of the excellent Hoomuz, King of Kings of Iran and Aniran, of the celestial race of Gods, grandson of the excellent Narses, King of Kings."

On the other side, the words are – "This is the figure of the adorer of Ormusd, the excellent Baraham, King of Kings of Iran and Aniran, sprung from the celestial race of Gods, son of the adorer of Ormusd, of the excellent Shapoor, King of Kings of Iran and Aniran, of the celestial race of Gods, grandson of the excellent Ormuz, King of Kings."

These inscriptions fix almost precisely the

æra of this excavation, and tend in some degree to give a date to the larger portion of the sculptures. The inscription to the right alludes to Shapoor, a king of the Sassanian dynasty, who died in the latter end of the fourth century: that to the left is to Baraham the Fourth, who, succeeding his elder brother, Shapoor the Third, was surnamed Kermanshah (Shah or King of Kerman), from having formerly been Viceroy of that province:—by him the city of Kermanshah was founded.

These two excavations appear to be so related to each other, that they may be considered as belonging to the same dynasty of kings: but I should be inclined to consider them as the productions of different periods, because the principal excavation, in which there is no inscription, is executed in a style infinitely superior to the other. Both are so much beyond the workmanship of the native artists in the Sassanian æra, that they must be productions of Grecian sculptors, many of whom were retained in the Persian court after the overthrow of the Seleucian dynasty in the East. The ball, or globular appearance observable in the head costume of the figures, in both excavations, belongs evidently to the race of the Sassanidæ, as may be seen by referring to the coins of that race of kings.

The larger excavation is said to have been made in the reign of the celebrated Chosroes, or Khosro Puviz, as he is called in Persian history; and, in the absence of more authentic information, I see no reason to doubt the accuracy of the tradition, as far as regards the period of the sculpture. Our guides attribute it to Furhaud, an Indian prince, who, they say, became so enamoured of the beautiful Shereen, that, unable to conquer his passion, he communicated the state of his feelings to her husband, Chosroes, and modestly requested that the king would yield up his lovely wife. Strange to say, though Chosroes was the most uxorious husband that ever flourished in Persian story, so great was his friendship for the young prince, that he consented to grant him his request, accompanied with this single condition, that, in testimony of his disinterested friendship, Furhaud would produce these specimens of art which I have endeavoured to describe.

There is a striking similitude in this relation and that of La Nouvelle Heloise. Here, as in the French tale, the love of Furhaud for this Oriental Julie is sanctioned by the husband. A slight discrepancy, however, occurs in this story, which puts in a much more generous light the sacrifice of the Persian, than that of the Swiss husband, Monsieur de Wolmar, who acquiesced in the affection of St. Preux for his lady, upon the understanding that it was to be conducted with the strictest regard to Platonic rules; while Chosroes, ignorant that such an individual, or his doctrine, ever existed, or doubtful of its efficacy, imposed only the conditions I have stated, before he would consent to resign the partner of his bosom to the arms of his friend.

The neighbourhood of the excavations is held in high veneration by the natives, as having been the retreat of Hajee Ibrahim Shah Zada, a royal hermit of great sanctity. A small low hut was pointed out to us as his cell. In the interior we saw a stone with a Cufic inscription. At a short distance were large heaps of stones, said to be the remains of an ancient city and temple of fire worshippers, but we could gain no further information respecting them.

After visiting the sculptures we retired to a tent, where we found a Persian breakfast prepared for us by Senor Oms. During the meal, a Persian dance was exhibited. The performer was supposed to personate a bride, though, in conformity to the depraved taste of the country, a boy twelve years old was her representative. Three musicians, with instruments more capable of making noise than producing melody, beat time to the dancer, whose motions were neither decent nor graceful, though our host and his native visitors seemed enraptured with the performance, and evinced their approbation by loud shouts of encouragement and clapping their hands. A hunch-backed player on the tambourine got so drunk that he was unable to proceed; so he was hoisted on a horse, behind one of the servants, and with his departure ended this disgusting performance.

We were witnesses to a more pleasing exhibition, in returning homeward: a mounted servant of Nasir Ali Meerza, one of the Prince's brothers, went past us at full gallop, and vaulting completely over the high peak of his Persian saddle, seated himself on the horse's neck, with his face towards its tail; then seizing his gun, which was slung at his back, he threw down his cap and fired at it;

the horse all the time going at full speed over uneven ground, strewed with loose stones and pieces of rock. The horse this man rode was of the Turcoman breed, which is here preferred to the Arabian. It is much taller than the Arab, standing generally from fifteen to sixteen hands; and in comparison with that beautiful animal appears to great disadvantage, both with respect to symmetry, and promise of strength or action. It has little bone, long legs, a spare carcase, and a large head out of all proportion with its body. Notwithstanding this unpromising appearance, the Turcoman is said to be capable of enduring very great fatigue, and the facility with which it ascends the most rugged eminences is astonishing. The plains in the neighbourhood of Kermanshah are supposed to be the same as those mentioned by Arrian* and Herodotus, as the country of the

* Arrian, Lib. 7, cap. 13.

Nissei, famous for its breed of horses. Here, according to Herodotus, one hundred and fifty thousand horses were accustomed to graze; but Arrian says that there were only five thousand when Alexander the Great came here, nearly all the rest having been stolen away. As there is no tale, however fabulous, in the Arabian Nights that has not some reference or allusion to reality, the fame of the cattle of this neighbourhood may have suggested to the mind of the author the story of the Winged Horse of Coordistan.

April 26.—The French officers accompanied us this morning on horseback, to make a survey of the town. We were attended by a considerable number of servants, armed with sticks, who led us through a succession of narrow streets, and at length brought us into the bazaar, which was at that time exceedingly crowded: here we were shocked to observe the use to which these batons were applied. Whenever our progress was in the least impeded by the crowd, the servants called out, "Make way for the Gentlemen!" and enforced their desire with the unremitting application of the stick, regardless of whom they struck, or where the blows fell. As we had reason to believe that this barbarous ceremony of Oriental despotism was intended as a compliment to us, we earnestly begged that the practice might be dispensed with on our account, as we could not but feel distressed at being the innocent instruments of such wanton barbarity. Our hosts ridiculed our scruples, upon the plea that it was the custom of the country, and our precursors continued to belabour the unresisting multitude as before. In the course of the ride, our consequence suffered a slight interruption. In turning one of the corners of the bazaar, we came suddenly on the retinue of the young Prince Tamas (Thomas) Meerza, governor of Hamadun, and a brother of Mohumud Hosein Meerza, who were pursuing the same measures to clear the way for his Highness; but so blind was the zeal of our lictors for the consequence of their masters, that the presence of royalty failed to arrest their attention, and the foremost of the Prince's attendants were favoured by a few marks of their unsparing regard. Our servants were thunderstruck on discovering their error; but our manifestations of respect to the Prince superseded the necessity of an explanation. The passengers enjoyed a momentary truce from this rencontre; the operation of clubs on both sides were suspended for the time; but the parties had no sooner got clear of each other, than hostilities upon the unfortunate crowd were again commenced with redoubled vigour.

April 27.—For the last two days, guns had been fired at intervals, preparatory to the removal of the late Prince's corpse for interment at Meshed Ali. This morning being appointed for the setting out of the *cortège*, we put crape on our left arms and sword-hilts, and mounting our horses, set off at an early hour, anxious to witness the n vel ceremony of a Prince's funeral procession two years after his decease.

As our eagerness to be in time brought us out much sooner than was necessary, we dismounted in a garden near the road-side, and whiled away a couple of hours in observing the various chatting parties around us, all dressed in black, their merry faces being somewhat curiously contrasted with their mournful garb.

Our attention to these groups was diverted by the appearance of a blind horseman of about sixty years of age; he was attended by a train of servants, one of whom held the rein of his bridle: upon inquiry we learned that he was a counsellor of the Prince's, by name Hassan Khan, to which was added the epithet of Khoord (the Blind), to distinguish him from the numerous courtiers of the same name.

In the brief interval of anarchy that, according to custom, followed the death of the late King,—Hassan Khan, at the head of what forces he could collect, became a competitor for the crown; but being conquered, was deprived of sight by order of his more successful rival.

A sudden discharge of cannon, followed by loud shrieks and lamentations, announced to us that the Prince had left the palace with the body of his father. We took our station near the gates of the town, ready to fall in with the procession. Near this place, riding a handsome charger, was Nasir Ali Meerza, the youngest son of the late Prince, a pretty boy of about five years old. His little Highness was attended by a pigmy train of courtiers of his own age and size, who seemed as well versed in the art of rendering homage, as their little lord and master was in receiving it; as for himself, he appeared to be quite indifferent either to the noise of the crowd or the occasion of it, all the time preserving a serious and dignified demeanour; and, as we approached him, he returned our salute with the easy air of one long accustomed to this sort of attention. But—little Highnesses are always great people. The Duc de Bourdeaux, a boy of the same age as the young Persian, when he reviewed his troops, was graciously pleased to compliment them on their skill in military evolutions; and the King of Rome, just escaped from the go-cart, reviewed the Marshals of France with that precocious dignity so inherent in royal progenies.

In the mean while the procession issued slowly out of the town, led by the artisans: each craft had with it a black banner, and a horse equipped in the same mournful trappings. Next came two men renowned for their strength, carrying a large brass ornament representing a palm-tree. After them two hundred Coordish soldiers, who were to escort the corpse to Meshed Ali: they wore blue jackets, cut in the European fashion, and the rest of their dress was according to the costume of the country. The escort was preceded by a corps of drums and fifes playing a variety of tunes, principally English: "Rule Britannia" was one; and there were several country dances. After the military, came the representatives of the Church—a large body of mounted Moolahs (priests), headed by their Bashee (chief), a jolly drunken-looking fellow, who, with a voice amounting to a scream, recited verses from a Koran, in which he was joined by his followers, who made the air resound with their vociferous lamentations. Behind them was the corpse of Mohumud Ali Meerza, borne by two mules, in that sort of covered litter called in Persian a *tukhte ruwaun*.

Immediately behind the corpse were Mohumud Hosein, the ruling Prince, and two of his brothers; the principal officers of the court closed the procession.

At intervals the cavalcade stopped, when every one, baring his breast, struck it so violently with his hand, that the flesh bore visible marks of the severity of the discipline: at these times the shouts were redoubled, and tears flowed copiously from every eye. Large groups of women, veiled from head to foot, and huddled together almost into shapeless heaps, were seated on each side of the road, and were by no means the least silent mourners of the party.

We fell in with the French officers in rear of the troops; two or three chiefs were in the same line with us. Immediately on my right was a handsome young man, whose eyes were red with weeping. He had been a favourite follower of the late Prince, for whom he had entertained a most sincere attachment; and I was beginning to sympathise with him in his sorrows, when it was insinuated that it was just possible wine, and not grief, had caused his tears to flow—a surmise that his subsequent behaviour in some degree warranted.

After proceeding about a mile, we quitted the procession, and halting on one side of the road, waited till the Prince had given us the *murukhus,* or permission to depart. His eyes were much inflamed, and tears chased each other down his cheeks. Thus far the ceremonial of grief had been conducted with the greatest propriety ; and any one witnessing the mournful demeanour of the Prince this morning, would have been impressed with a high opinion of his filial piety. The day closed on a scene of a very different description. The funeral procession arrived at Mahidesht near sunset, when his Highness ordered the caravanserai to be cleared of its inmates, and, taking with him several boon companions, this sorrowing son passed the night in drinking and singing, determined to keep his father's *wake* in the true Irish fashion, and, if any grief or care remained, to drown it in the bowl. The following morning, these merry mourners remounted their horses, and reached Kermanshah without accident; though the Prince was so intoxicated, that on arriving at the palace-gate he fell off his horse into the arms of his attendants, and was by them conveyed to his own apartment in a state of drunken insensibility.

Foremost on the list of persons selected by his Highness to assist him in the celebration of these funeral orgies, was the Moolahi Bashee, once his tutor, and now his associate in every species of debauchery. He who as chief of the religion had, in the day, with weeping eyes and melancholy howl, sung the requiem to the soul of the father, was, in the night, administering *spiritual* consolation to that of the son. He who, in the morning, chaunted verses from that book which inculcates wine as an abomination, was, in the evening, so overcome by its influence, as to be scarcely able to hiccup out the licentious songs* of his country.

The person from whom we received this information was likewise one of the party; no other than Suleiman Khan, the chieftain whose grief had attracted my attention at the funeral. We were sitting after dinner in the evening, when this person, in the same "suit of solemn black" as of the preceding day, staggered into the room. Interrupting his relation here and there with an occasional roar of laughter, he described to us those scenes of revelry of which he had been so willing a participator.

Suleiman Khan, surnamed Kuruzungeer,

* Some Persian love-songs have been elegantly translated into English by one of the most flowery poets of the last century; but the reader would throw down the verses with disgust, if he was aware of the objects to whom these amatory effusions are generally addressed.

is chief of a tribe of twelve thousand Coords, the best foot-soldiers in the Persian dominions. They are not Mahometans, but of a peculiar sect called Ali Illahi, that is, Ali is of God. They acknowledge Christ as the Messiah, but believe that he appeared on earth a second time in the person of Ali. They practise circumcision, but not as a religious rite. As dissenters from the established religion of a country are generally viewed with more dislike than those who deny its tenets altogether, so these believers in Ali are held in greater abhorrence, by his other disciples, than either Jews or Christians. Our anxiety to proceed homewards induced us to decline a very pressing solicitation from Suleiman, to visit him in his own country; which I now much regret, as this tribe is described as having many curious customs that would have amply repaid our inquiries.

Although Suleiman Khan holds a despotic

sway over his own tribe, it has not exempted him from the casualties incidental to the follower of a Persian court. By Mohumud Ali Meerza he was condemned to death for an unsuccessful attack on a fort, and only pardoned at the intercession of Monsieur De Veaux. By order of the ruling Prince he was so severely bastinadoed as to be unable to walk for six weeks. Thus, with the vicissitudes of an Oriental life, this mighty despot of a tribe becomes the unfortunate victim of a torture, inflicted at the will or caprice of one who, the moment before, was the social partner of his revels.

CHAPTER III.

Misunderstanding between Messrs. Court and De Veaux—Conduct of Señor Oms—Reconciliation between our Hosts—Moolah Ali's opinion of Duelling—Second interview with the Prince—Departure from Kermanshah—Unsuccessful Expedition into the Mountains—Pic-nic Breakfast—We take leave of Messrs. Court and De Veaux—Be-sitoon—Bas-reliefs—Sahanah—Concobar—Visit the Governor—Temple of Diana.

April 30—*May* 1.—We were now all ready to proceed on our journey. The preparations for the funeral of the late Prince, which had for some days past put a stop to all public business, had prevented our procuring a *rukum*, or order, from the Prince, to proceed unmolested, and to be supplied with whatever we might require on the road; the whole population between Kermanshah and Hamadan consisting, equally with that through which we had passed, of hordes of robbers. With the assistance of Moolah Ali, we obtained this document; and our arrangements being completed, we intended to have resumed our journey on the following morning, when a circumstance occurred which occasioned a farther delay.

In the course of conversation after supper this evening, a misunderstanding took place between our hosts. In consequence of this, Monsieur De Veaux left the house at daylight the next morning (May 1), and at eight o'clock a challenge had been offered and accepted in due form by the parties, who agreed to meet with pistols the morning after our departure.

As we had been present at the whole transaction, we drew up a letter, declaring it our opinion that nothing had occurred to justify the proceeding. We were at a loss where to send our dispatch, as M. De Veaux, conjecturing our interference, had concealed his abode from us. In this dilemma, Señor Oms, under pretence of becoming a mediator, took charge of our letter: which he suppressed, and instead of attempting a reconciliation, did every thing to foment the quarrel between Monsieur De Veaux and his former friend. The motives for this conduct were as diabolical as they were dastardly—a most inveterate hatred towards both parties, which, in case of either falling, would have been gratified.

Failing in his attempt, and fearing the effect of our endeavours at a reconciliation, he tried to perpetrate with his own hand, what he had hoped would have been done by that of another. In the evening, as we were seated at dinner, this Spanish ruffian, attended by a body of soldiers, rushed into the room, uttered the most dreadful imprecations, and drawing his dagger, motioned his men to advance. As his object was evidently assassination, we deemed it high time to interfere, so, making a charge towards the door, we succeeded in routing the enemy, many of whom we obliged to go the shortest way down stairs, but, owing to the crowd beneath, without detriment to a single neck. As for the leader, he was content to walk out of the door, particularly as we intimated, that, if he demurred, the window would be the exit we should select for him.

May 2.—Early in the morning, we went to Monsieur De Veaux, whom we found encamped two miles from the town. We recapitulated the events of the evening, and at last succeeded in bringing him home with us, and effecting a reconciliation between himself and Monsieur Court; a matter of some difficulty, as each had been successful in more than one fatal rencontre, and had, under Napoleon, imbibed those absurd prejudices so prevalent in that army, and which, half a century ago, was the bane of society in England and the sister kingdom ; but which have now happily given place to better feelings, and truer notions of honour.

The pitch to which duelling had at one time been carried, by the European officers in the service of the late Prince of Kermanshah, at once excited his astonishment and alarm. It was in vain that he threatened the survivor with death, or tried by ridicule to do away with a custom which threatened to leave his little army entirely without officers.

We were considerably amused by the observations on the subject of duelling of our friend Moolah Ali, whose notions of honour somewhat resembled those set down in Falstaff's catechism.

"How foolish," said he, "is it for a man

who wishes to kill his enemy, to expose his own life, when he can accomplish his purpose with so much greater safety, by shooting at him from behind a rock!"

Our hosts being determined to represent the conduct of Señor Oms to the Prince, requested us to accompany them, to give evidence if it should be necessary. As the French officers have at all times access to his Highness, we were admitted without scruple into the garden of the palace, and an officer of the household went to inform his Highness of our wish to have an audience. While here, our attention was arrested by hearing some one, at a short distance, singing, or rather screaming a song with all the power of his lungs. In spite of the drunken hiccup, which occasionally interrupted the harmony, we thought we could recognize the voice of the Moolahi Bashee, occupied, when last we heard it, in chaunting the requiem of the Prince's father: we were not mistaken, his Highness, not liking the rigours of the solemn fast of Ramazan, had invited a few friends to partake of a social bowl, and, among others, this holy man, who doubtless procured them a dispensation. The sudden silence of the chorister proved to us that our arrival had been announced; and as we were admitted to the presence, we observed him, with two or three effeminate-looking boys, stealing down one of the avenues.

The Prince was standing with his back against a tree, and, supported by a stick, was trying to conceal the impression the wine had made on his brain. Señor Oms had been sent for, and arrived shortly after. There were present at the interview, Assiz Khan, a young Coordish nobleman, and Hassan Khan Khoord, the blind counsellor whom we had seen at the funeral. Messieurs Court and De Veaux having related all the circumstances of the case, Señor Oms attempted a justification, but was interrupted by Hassan Khan

Khoord, who used the expression *Koor Khoordeed*, a Persian term of reproach, for which the propriety of our language has no synonym. During this interview, we were frequently appealed to, respecting the truth of the French officers' statement, and just as we concluded in confirmation of what they had said, we were somewhat startled at the Prince's saying to us, "*Eedn keh Gofteed deroogh neest?*"—Is not that which you have told me a lie?—a harsh sound to an English ear, but in this land of falsehood, a mere idiomatical phrase of inquiry. Our conference ended with Señor Oms being sent to prison, and the Prince resuming those enjoyments which we had so unseasonably interrupted.

May 3.—Our negotiations between the belligerent powers having been brought to a happy termination, we had nothing now to detain us at Kermanshah, so, having our mules laden, we bade adieu to this city, and once more found ourselves on the road. The next halting-place was Hamadan, four days' journey hence, and the seat of government of Tamas Meerza, brother to the Prince of Kermanshah. The country lying between these two towns is the most mountainous of all Irak. It is called by the natives Il Jebal (the mountainous), and is supposed to be the Matiene mentioned by Greek and Roman authors.

Wishing to give another day to the examination of the sculptures at Tauk Bostaun, we proceeded thither in company with our friends Messrs. Court and De Veaux, and two or three Persians. In the evening, we all dined together on the banks of the stream, which supplied us plentifully with fish, and we passed the time in high glee till a late hour; when the excavation furnished us with a classical night's lodging: and, with a rock for a pillow, we slept soundly till the bright light of the sun warned us of the return of day.

May 4.—We devoted this day to an unsuccessful expedition into the mountains, having been deluded into a hope of finding some antiquities by the account given us, that four miles hence was a cave full of statues and inhabited by genii, who suffered no person to return alive, who dared to penetrate their enchanted abode. After an hour's painful climbing up a steep and rugged mountain, we came to the mouth of the dreaded cavern, which we entered, having been provided with lights. It was very spacious, and composed entirely of stalactites, produced by infiltration, which would exhibit the appearance of statues, when viewed from without; but fear had so long predominated over curiosity, that no native had ever dared to solve the mystery, though tradition had long given a celebrity to this place.

A good pic-nic breakfast compensated in some measure for our disappointment. A Persian, who was of the party, regardless of the solemn fast ordained by his creed, or the interdiction of wine, ate much, and drank more; but we had seen too many votaries of Bacchus among the Mussulmans to be any longer astonished at their debaucheries; being now fully convinced that a true believer may be as great a toper as any Christian infidel.

May 5.—This day's march was to Besitoon, a place celebrated for ancient sculptures, and supposed to be the Bagistana of Diodorus Siculus and Isidorus of Charax. Having sent forward our servants and baggage two hours before us, we stayed to breakfast with our kind European friends, who accompanied us half way on our day's march. We cannot speak in too high terms of the kindness and hospitality we experienced from these officers. During our stay at Kermanshah, every wish had been anticipated, and for the time we remained under their roof, they seemed to have forgotten their own pursuits, and to have studied only what would be most conducive to our interests and comforts.

We traversed the base of the mountain for eight miles in an easterly direction, after which, we turned to the north; here we met a numerous tribe of Illyauts marching with their tents and mules: they had just arrived from Arabia, and were about to take up their quarters for the summer season in this neighbourhood.

Six miles from Be-sitoon, at a short distance on our right, we saw the capitals and bases of some pillars, which may be well worthy the attention of any traveller following the same track: indeed it was much to be regretted that our time did not permit us to examine them more minutely, as we might have ascertained the order of their architecture, and have given a clue, that should fix some era to the antiquities of Be-sitoon, which, up to the present moment, are matters of doubtful speculation.

Mr. Macdonald Kinneir supposes the word Be-sitoon to be derived from the Persian negative particle *be,* and the word *sitoon,* signifying no pillars; but it is possible that the pillars seen by us, might have given the name to the city, as Beest-sitoon, signify twenty pillars: in the same manner the ruins of Persepolis are called Chehel-sitoon, or forty pillars.

We reached our destination at five o'clock in the afternoon, passed the caravanserai and villages, and pitched our tents on the banks of a rivulet, at the base of the stupendous rock of Be-sitoon, which forms an abrupt termination to the mountain chain bounding the valley of Kermanshah to the north.

According to Diodorus Siculus, Semiramis, in her march from Babylon to Ecbatana, the capital of Media, halted at the foot of a high mountain called Bagistan,* and there made a

* Dio. Sic. Wess. Lib. i. p. 126. In the Byzantian History, mention is made of the city as well as of the mountain of Bagistana, Βαγισταvα πολις της Μηδιας και ορyος Βαγισταvov. τὸ ἐθvικov Βαγισταvος.

Bagistan is derived from the Persian words *bāg* and *stan*, signifying a region of gardens.

garden twelve furlongs in circumference, which was watered by a large fountain. Be-sitoon will answer in most respects to this description: it is situated in the direct road from Babylon to Hamadan, the supposed site of Ecbatana; the high mountain of Be-sitoon will correspond with Bagistan, which is described as seventeen furlongs in height. The plain is well capable of cultivation, and is watered by a stream which issues from the rock. The same author informs us, that a piece was cut out of the lower part of the rock, where Semiramis caused to be sculptured her own image, surrounded by a hundred of her guards. An immense portion of the rock has evidently been scarped out, qut, after the most minute examination, we are of opinion that no figures can ever have existed, though this has evidently been the commencement of some great undertaking.

As Diodorus Siculus did not see the sculpture he describes, may it not be possible that it was never farther advanced than the scarp-ed portion of the rock before us? Indeed scepticism may fairly be allowed to exist on any subject concerning Semiramis, when eight authors, who have written respecting this famous queen, differ as to the time in which she lived, upwards of fifteen hundred years. But, putting the sculpture of Semiramis out of the question, the works at Be-sitoon bear marks of the most remote antiquity.

At the foot of the mountain is an extensive burying-ground, a proof of the former exist-ence of population in this neighbourhood; many of the tomb-stones are of white marble, having inscriptions beautifully cut in the Sy-riac and Cufic characters. We found among them the fragment of a white marble pillar; the shaft appears to have been formed of one stone; the base and capital were in different parts of the burying ground, both richly sculptured. On the capital is the figure of a king, in rich robes; and I would willingly, in the absence of her hundred guards, have attributed this beautiful pillar to Semiramis, who, according to Isidorus of Charax, erected one at Bagistan; but candour obliges me to add, that from the resemblance of the ornaments to those on the Tauk Bostaun sculptures, I cannot fix a more ancient date than the Sassanian era.

May 6.—We devoted this day to the examination of the sculptures, commencing from the west. The first object that arrested our attention was a large tablet, with an Arabic inscription, on the face of the rock, at about the height of twenty feet. On approaching this for examination, our interest was strongly excited by the appearance of two lines in Greek characters, forming part of an inscription, which we were mortified to find had been nearly obliterated to make way for this modern record, relating to a grant of land to the neighbouring caravanserai. In the imperfect record before us, we thought we could decypher the name of a person called Gotars, or Gobars, who was probably a Satrap, as that word twice occurs in the imperfect relic spared to us by the Arab barbarian. Who this Satrap was, whose deeds were thought worthy of such a memorial, it is difficult to determine.

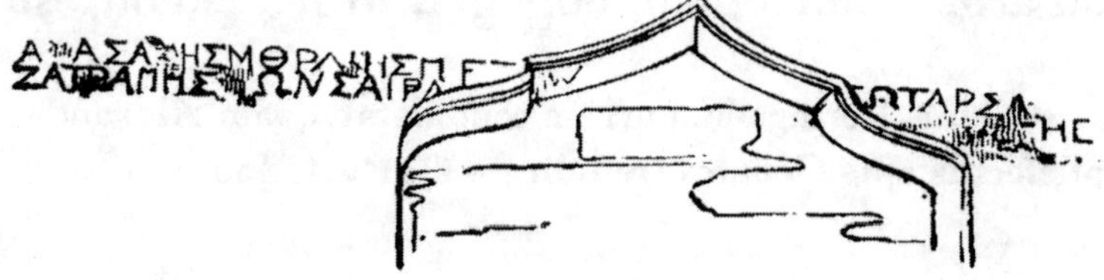

Quintus Curtius mentions that a prefect of Persagada, by name Gobares, delivered up that city to Alexander the Great.* Had Gobares been at Bagistan, he might have helped us out in the application of the inscription.

As a second conjecture I may add, that among the Kings of Persia I find the name of the third of the second dynasty of the Parthian race was Goters: nothing more is recorded of him—*stat nominis umbra.*

Below the inscription, we found the remains of a group of figures in low relief: after repeated examination at different periods of the day, and availing ourselves of the most favourable lights, we discovered (what appears to have escaped the notice of preceding travellers) a winged female figure, hovering in the air, in the act of crowning with a wreath an armed horseman, engaged in fierce contest

* Cyrus Persagadam urbem condiderat, quam Alexandro præfectus ejus Gobares tradidit. Q. Curt. Lib. v. cap. 6.

with another similarly accoutred and mounted. Both have their spears in rest, on the point of attack. On the left, some animal appears to be running away. The figures of the bas-relief were so much in proportion, and the general outline was so good, that, without the inscription, I should have attributed the work to Grecian artists.

Proceeding eastward, we saw in a chasm of the mountain, at a great height, another bas-relief; which, from its general resemblance to the sculptures of Persepolis, may be considered as coeval with those splendid specimens of ancient workmanship. This our guides called the Dervisham (Dervishes), but were not as usual prepared with a tradition respecting it: not so a certain French traveller, who has published an account of this sculpture, and gravely asserts it to represent our Saviour and the twelve Apostles.

It consists of a group of thirteen figures, appearing to represent two attendants presenting ten captives to their king, who is seated above in robes of state: one prisoner is lying on his back with his hands raised, in the act of imploring mercy, while a female figure, who stands near, is looking with a most piteous aspect, apparently seconding the supplication of the fallen captive. The general has his right foot standing on the prisoner's breast. The remaining nine figures, among which is the female, have their hands tied behind their backs, and they are fastened by the necks to each other with a rope. The figures, at the distance from whence we viewed them, appeared about two feet high; the captives are dressed apparently in the costume of different tribes, and the last in the string has the high Coordish cap. On each side of the group, and immediately below it, are eight large compartments, covered with writing in the Babylonian character, which proves, beyond the slightest shadow of a doubt, their antiquity. Sir Robert Porter thinks that this bas-relief alludes to the Babylonish captivity. But for the female captive, I should be of the same opinion. In many particulars, the Scripture account of Esther pleading before Ahasuerus, in behalf of her Jewish brethren, is strongly illustrated in this sculpture.

We started for Sahanah, a distance of sixteen miles, at eight o'clock in the evening. A quarter of a mile from Be-sitoon, on our left hand, we saw, by the light of the moon, some mounds which we were told had been a field fortification thrown up by Nadir Shah: the works appeared to be extensive, but we were too full of ancient relics to interest ourselves in the works of this modern conqueror.

The road led through a fertile and well irrigated valley, flooded in many parts from the overflowings of the water-courses. An hour after midnight we reached our destination; and not liking the wretched appearance of the caravanserai, encamped outside the walls of the town.

Sahanah is situate at the base of one of the lofty ranges of mountains. As in most Persian towns, its houses are in a dilapidated state. It is somewhat larger than the generality of those through which we have passed; and the surrounding gardens give an agreeable appearance, which does not correspond with the actual state of the place.

Curiosity brought numbers of the inhabitants round us this morning. They were inoffensive, and seated themselves in picturesque groups in the neighbourhood of the tents. Like the natives of all this country, they are professional robbers.

We commenced our march to Concovar, another sixteen mile stage, at half-past three in the afternoon; having been induced to travel by daylight, at the suggestion of the French officers, who had advised us to reach a narrow defile in the mountains before dark, as it was a plàce where robbers were in the habit of issuing forth and attacking the caravans. We continued for two hours traversing a spacious plain, in a S. E. direction. This brought us to the ascent of a steep and stony mountain. At six o'clock, we passed the narrow defilè in the mountains, without an adventure. To judge from the appearances of the pass, it is well adapted for the purposes to which robbers appropriate it.

After descending for an hour, we entered a well-cultivated valley; and, at ten, arrived at the town of Concovar. By the imperfect light of the moon, we observed the remains of a splendid temple, supposed to have been dedicated to Diana. Our chief muleteer, not liking the trouble of unpacking the tents, assured us the caravanserais were very comfortable; but, as our ideas of comfort differed materially from his, we fixed upon a field near the Governor's house for our encampment. We had scarcely begun to unload our mules, when we received a peremptory order from the Governor to go into the town, on account of the robbers; though I know not whether his command proceeded from the fear that we were of the fraternity, or that he was anxious for our safety. In this dilemma we produced the Prince's *rukum*, and, instead of being obliged to comply with the injunction, we were furnished by the Governor with a guard of ten men.

We had intended to have resumed our journey this afternoon, but Baba Khan, the Governor, sent his Mehmaundaur to say that he would not allow us to travel, except by day, as numerous hordes of banditti infested the road we were to pass, and that, in compliance with the Prince's *rukum*, he was obliged to provide for our safety, whether we liked or not. After breakfast we called upon this personage: he was attended by a numerous suite, dressed, for the most part, in the Persian costume; though we observed one or two young men whose turbans showed they were Turks, detained probably as pledges for the good behaviour of some of their relations, who, like the hostages at Kermanshah, may have sought the precarious protection of Persia from the persecution of their own tyrants.

In the interview with the Governor, we had no reason to be flattered with the cordiality of our reception. After coldly bidding us welcome, a silence of some minutes elapsed, unbroken by his attendants; he then stammered out some common-place compliment, and fell to muttering to himself a string of prayers, it being deemed an act highly meritorious for a Mussulman to invoke the deity in the presence of infidels. We had neither pipes nor coffee, on account of the Ramazan; and we were not sorry to shorten our visit, after obtaining a promise that a person should be sent with us to show us the temple. and to protect us from insult; but as this man never came, we set out accompanied by two of our own servants.

This temple is of the Doric order of architecture, comprising a square of two hundred and fifty paces. To the West, the bases of ten, and a portion of the shafts of eight pillars remain standing; these are from six to seven feet high: the pillars measure from four feet eight to four feet nine inches in diameter, and fourteen feet eleven inches in circumference; the basement is formed of large blocks from six to nine feet in length. The whole building is of greyish white veined marble; huge fragments of pillars lay scattered in every direction, and the stones seem marked as if to prevent their being displaced. The natives, who attribute this temple to the work of Genii, say that it had once four hundred pillars; but they have no tradition that could lead to its history; however, its name Concovar, or, as it might be pronounced with equal propriety, Concobar,* is conclusive evidence, that here is the site of the ancient town of that name, mentioned by Isidorus of Charax, and that these are the ruins of the celebrated temple sacred to Diana.

While we were taking the dimensions of the temple, a crowd of four or five hundred people had collected and began hooting us; calling us dogs, shebres, infidels, and many untranslateable epithets of abuse, in which their language is very copious. Not content with this, they pelted us with stones, and showed every mark of hostility. Our Turkish attendants, being both dressed in the garb of their country, and consequently equal objects of hatred with our-

* The b and v in Persian, are constantly used for each other: one instance will suffice—the plural of the word na-eeb, a viceroy, is equally pronounced nu-vaub, and nubaub, or, according to our pronunciation, *nabob*.

selves, came in for a share of the attack. These, not so patient as we were, rushed in amongst the crowd, and used their large sticks, with a rancour which a religious difference of opinion unfortunately but too often generates for ourselves; we continued our measurements, though the counting paces was occasionally interrupted by fragments of the temple being unceremoniously rolled at our feet. On returning to our tents, we were followed by the crowd, now considerably encreased; when one of the Governor's people came forward, and called out to them to disperse,—an order which was immediately obeyed; and a sudden silence succeeded to the unpleasant discord with which we had been regaled for the last hour. As all our annoyances had arisen from the Governor's not having sent the person he promised, we intimated to him that we should make a representation of his conduct to the King, who he well knew would have been happy for a pretext to extort money. This message brought his Mehmaundaur, with a submissive apology; so we sent him some tea, for which he had begged, as an earnest of our forgiveness, and here the matter ended: we were assured, however, that the fear of injuring persons travelling with the Prince's *rukum*, alone prevented the inhabitants from assassinating the whole party.

Concovar is the frontier town of a tribe, and forms a kind of head-quarters to one of the most desperate gangs which infest these mountains; so, all things considered, we have reason to congratulate ourselves on having got so well out of the adventure.

May 9.—After all our troubles in the inhospitable neighbourhood of Concovar, we were not sorry to quit the sulky Governor and his riotous adherents; but, as every one here seemed determined to thwart us, we were delayed an hour by the impertinence of the master of the caravanserai, who refused to let our mules go till we sent him a present. We once more sent to the Governor, and begged he would send one of his attendants with our servants, and cause the master of the caravanserai to be brought before us and bastinadoed in our presence; but this fellow no sooner perceived the Governor's servant, than, as many a man has done before him, off he scampered, to escape the fangs of justice.

CHAPTER IV.

Sadawar—Our Host and his two Wives—Hamadan—A Chupper, or Courier—Hajee Abbas, the Prince's Mehmaundaur—Dispensation from the Fast—Ancient Inscription—Elwund—Morning Visitors—The Prince's Physician—His Eulogium on Sir John Malcolm—The Rabbi of the Jews—Chief of the Armenians—A Persian in pursuit of the Philosopher's Stone—High respect for the English Character.

At seven in the morning we commenced our march to Sadawar. We first ascended a stony pass, which led into an extensive plain of an oval form to the North. We then passed through one of the numerous villages which lie scattered over the valley; and three hours from the pass in the mountains, reached the village of Sadawar, seated at the base of the Elwund mountain, which forms the northern boundary of the valley. This village, or rather town, contains four hundred houses, and has a governor appointed by the King. While looking at the Serai, which we found to be very inconvenient, we accepted the offer of one of the inhabitants to take up our quarters with him, and took possession of the verandah of his house. Our new host was a man about sixty years of age: he had two wives—one a comely woman of eighteen years of age, and the other ten; they looked cheerful and contented, and, if we may judge from the manner in which they performed their domestic duties, seemed not to regard the disparity of years between themselves and their joint husband.

May 10.—We set out this morning at six for Hamadan, having a high mountain to cross, and a long march before us. In three quarters of an hour we reached the base of the Elwund, the Mount Orontes of Diodorus Siculus. The ascent, which is very steep and circuitous, occupied an hour, and proved very distressing to our cattle; large masses of snow lay in ravines near the top in every direction, over which the wind blew painfully cold. The western face of the mountain was covered with aromatic shrubs, which wafted a delightful fragrance through the air. The descent on the eastern side is gradual, but the road is much broken by streams of water supplied by the melting of the snow. Near the base of the mountain we passed a caravanserai: the centre was roofed in at the top, different from these buildings in general, and a very necessary protection against the severe cold in this mountainous region during the winter season. Bands of robbers have at different times occupied the building, and converted into a place of molestation to the traveller what had been built for his protection. We passed a fountain at the bottom of the pass, which the muleteer informed us was a common post for robbers to waylay passengers; they sometimes collected together to the number of thirty or forty, and laid the largest caravans under contribution. We had now been long accustomed to be in a state of readiness for attack, and our little band preserved as good an order of march as the nature of its force admitted; though we had occasion to regret the loss of our former intelligent muleteer, who, when any danger was to be apprehended, evinced a foresight and circumspection that in a great measure relieved us from the trouble of caution on our own part. At present, our attention was constantly employed to prevent the muleteer from allowing the cattle to stray.

The whole mountain to the summit was clothed with rich verdure, chiefly aromatic herbs of great variety, to gather which, people come from all quarters, and even from India. We met here two natives of that country, who had travelled thus far to cull the simples, which they apply to medical purposes.

After descending the mountain, we traversed along its base in a S. E. direction, crossing numerous rills, the waters of which assist in irrigating the fruitful valley of Hamadan. Immediately on quitting the precipices of the mountain, we entered upon well-cultivated land, which extended to the city. Two miles from Hamadan, we passed a considerable stream of water, by a neat stone bridge. Near it were many marble tombstones, elegantly sculptured in flowers and inscriptions in the Cufic and Arabic characters. Hence the road led through gardens surrounded by walls, extending to the town. We had sent a servant in advance with the *rukum* to the Vizier, and made the same request as on entering Kermanshah—to be allowed to occupy a garden or empty house within the walls of the town. Awaiting his return, we entered a garden by the road-side. Numbers of people were at work in the different fields around us, chiefly employed in manuring and dressing the vine. After remaining a considerable time, we became impatient, and proceeded onwards.

Fragments of ancient buildings met our view as we entered upon the site of the once renowned capital of Media; but we felt too much fatigued, from a long march of eleven hours, the greater part of the time under the influence of a burning sun, to bestow much attention on antiquities. As our servant had taken a different direction from that by which we entered, we had to wander about for a considerable time without any person to direct us, and were at the same time obliged to encounter the impertinent scrutiny of nearly the whole population, whom curiosity had gathered in crowds around us. Our servant at length returned; and from him we learned that, instead of an empty house, Tamas Meerza, the Prince of Hamadan, had ordered his Vizier to have the Mehmaun Khoneh prepared for our reception, and had desired that his Mehmandaur, Hajee Abbas, should wait upon us, to see that we were supplied with whatever we might require, his Highness wishing that we should be considered as his guests during our stay.

Our new quarters are comprised in a building within a large enclosed space, protected by a square wall, which is flanked at each angle by protruding bastions; the interior of the dwelling is fitted up with nummuds and carpets, the usual articles of furniture in a Persian apartment. I must not except a large chafing-dish, with a sparkling fire, in the centre of the room, round which we were glad to assemble; for the evening was as cold as the day had been hot, and reminded us that this elevated spot had been selected, from the coolness of the atmosphere, as the summer residence of the Assyrian Kings.

Besides our own party, there was another public guest in the Mehmaun Khonah, Mohumud Hassan, one of the King's chuppers or messengers: this man had left Kermanshah only the morning before, and arrived a short time before us at this place,—a journey of one hundred and twenty miles, over a very mountainous country, on one horse. As there are no relays, or post-houses, in this part of the Persian territories, the next morning, he mounted on the same animal, and resumed his journey to Teheraun, two hundred miles distant, expecting to reach it on the second day.

Till within these few years, the only modes of communication between the capital of Persia and her provinces, were either by one of these mounted couriers, or by cassids, foot-messengers. A chupper seldom changes his horse; generally going a steady amble at the rate of about four or five miles an hour: some have been known to go from Teheraun to Bushire, a distance of seven hundred miles, in the space of ten days. Of late, a post establishment has been formed between Teheraun and the frontier of Russia; but, like many other royal establishments, it is farmed out to some noblemen of the court, and has consequently been subject to very great abuses.

As Messrs. Hart and Lamb wished to continue their journey to Tabriz by the mountains of Curdistan, and as Mr. Hamilton and myself were anxious to visit the court of Persia, we agreed to separate at this place, and to meet again at Tabriz, whence we thought to resume our journey together. Leaving Messrs Hart and Lamb to make their own arrangements, Mr. Hamilton and myself availed ourselves of the assistance of Mohumud Hassan, and by him dispatched a letter that had been given us by the Governor of Bombay to Major Willock, the British chargé-d'affaires, together with a few lines from ourselves, informing him of our intended visit to the Capital.

May 11.—It was our intention to have paid our respects to the Vizier, but he was unwell; and as he could not see us himself, he sent the Mehmaundaur Hajee Abbas with a message, welcoming us to Hamadan, in the name of the Prince. We found Hajee Abbas an agreeable man, and tolerably well versed in the literature of his country. Of this he gave us abundant proofs; for we could scarcely ask any question, to which we did not receive in answer a quotation of some dozen lines from Hafiz or Sadi. The Hajee was at this time suffering from a stomachic complaint, brought on by an excessive use of opium; this he felt the more severely on account of Ramazan, which did not permit him to eat or drink while the sun was above the horizon. To soften the rigours of fasting, he had been in the habit of spending the day in bed; but he hoped that the English physician would give him instant relief. Mr. Lamb answered, that a disease of several years' standing could not be cured in a day; and, as preliminary to recovery, he must not fast so much. This advice was no sooner given, than off went the Hajee to order something for dinner; first taking the precaution to call his servant to witness the agreeable order given by the Hakeem. The success of Hajee Abbas in eluding the law of the Koran, brought a number of applicants for medical advice, apparently for the sole purpose of procuring a similar dispensation.

We made an excursion to the Elwund this afternoon, to see an inscription on the face of the mountain, an hour's ride from the town, in a southerly direction, along a road leading to Kermanshah. The inscription is cut in a large mass of coarse-grained granite, on the face of the hill to the West of the road, whence it is visible. There are two separate tablets, each divided into three compartments: one containing twenty, and the other twenty-one lines of writing, in the simplest form of the Babylonian character. From being in a sheltered situation, the inscription has undergone little change from the weather: but we did not take a copy of it, which would have occupied a considerable time; understanding from our guides, that one had been already made by Sir John Malcolm. This inscription is called by the natives Gunge Namah, the history of the treasure which they say is buried near this spot; but that it will never be discovered till some one shall be fortunate enough to decypher the mysterious writing. Then, like the magic "Sesame," which afforded entrance to the den of the Forty Thieves, this mountain will reveal to the translator its hidden treasures. Our guides informed us, that there were some remains of an ancient structure on the top of this mountain, built by a son of Solomon, who, they say, gave name to the mountain.

The Orontes is celebrated over all the

East, for its natural as well as supernatural properties. Many of the natives told us that there were several ores of silver and gold in the mountain, but that no one would take the trouble to work them, as the produce of their labours would go either to the King, or to the Prince Governor of Hamadan. Its vegetable productions are, as I said before, so good, that people from every country come to gather them; and the belief is general here, that there is a certain grass which has the power of changing every metal into gold; added to which, this mountain is supposed to contain that long sought object of cupidity, the philosopher's stone.

May 12.—All our morning was occupied in receiving visitors. Amongst them was the Prince's physician, a respectable-looking old man, of very amiable manners, possessing a degree of liberality of opinion and general information rarely to be met with in one of the shallow pretenders to medicine in this country. His visit was principally directed to Mr. Lamb, whose fame as a physician had travelled before him to this place. Our visitor sat with us nearly the whole morning; but he was so intelligent and entertaining, that we could not find fault with the length of his stay. As a proof of his modesty, he acknowledged the superiority of European medical knowledge, by consulting Mr. Lamb on the state of his own health, and by receiving medicine from him; but what pleased us most, was the honourable mention he made of Sir John Malcolm, with whom he appears to have been well acquainted; and our national vanity was much gratified by the admiration he professed for our highly gifted countryman.

Perhaps no man ever employed on a foreign mission has done more to exalt the character of his country than has this distinguished individual. The name of Malcolm is familiar to every one in the countries through which he has travelled, and all persons express the same unbounded respect for his talents and character; his name, indeed, secures kindness for his countrymen throughout Persia.

In the course of the morning a Rabbi of the Jews came to pay us a visit. From him we heard a most affecting detail of the persecution exercised by the Mahometans towards his unhappy people: the whole tenor of his language was that of bitter lamentation; and he spoke of their suffering with a degree of freedom, before the Mussulman doctor, that despair only could have dictated. It is not, said he, of the oppression of one tyrant alone that we complain; for we are subject not only to the iron grasp of the government, but, on account of our religious tenets, are exposed to the avarice and cruelty of every petty professor of authority.

The Rabbi informed us that the number of his people amounted to four hundred houses. The tombs of Mordecai and Esther are cherished here, amidst their misery; and the expectation of the promised Messiah is the hope that enables them to sustain the load of oppression which would be otherwise insupportable.

Every circumstance connected with the state of the Jews of this place is of important interest. Ecbatana is mentioned in Scripture as one of the cities in which the Jews were placed at the time of the captivity, and it is possible that the present inhabitants may be the descendants of the tribe who occupied the city under the Babylonian yoke.

While our interest was strongly excited by this account of a scattered remnant of Israel, the chief of the Armenians came with an offering of two large flasks of wine, which this Eastern Christian had brought to ensure a favourable reception from his more fortunate brethren. His detail was equally affecting with that of the Rabbi; here the unbelieving Jew and Christian dog are alike subject to the oppression of the intolerant Mussulman.

Our next visitor was a native of rank, who had expended the greater part of his fortune in search of the philosopher's stone: the ill-success he had hitherto met with, so far from discouraging him in his pursuit, seemed only to have encreased his ardour. The object of his present visit was to consult Mr. Lamb, whom he believed to be in possession of the secret. He entertained this opinion, in consequence of being told by some one who had been with us, that the learned Englishman was examining stones, and subjecting them to a chemical process. This was true enough; Mr. Lamb being a geologist had been so employed, and the stones and chemical tests lying still upon the table served thoroughly to confirm our visitor in this conviction, which no assurances we could at first give had the power of removing. Finding Mr. Lamb what he deemed obdurate in withholding the desired information, he seized a bottle of acid, with which he had seen him produce effervescence with limestone; and thinking this phial would open to him the wished-for treasure, implored in the most piteous accent that it might be given him.

We gathered from his conversation, that he had been made the dupe of one of those artful impostors common in this country, who go about preying on the credulity and weakness of those whose avarice make them easy victims. We informed him that many years ago, the principal philosophers of Europe had been engaged in this visionary pursuit, which had now for upwards of a century been abandoned, from a conviction of its being unattainable; and we strongly advised him, on the next visit he received from his philosopher, to satisfy all further demands by a vigorous application of the bastinado. After an hour's conversation we appeared to have succeeded in somewhat staggering his belief, and his countenance on leaving us conveyed the impression that he would attend to our suggestion.

The belief, universally entertained throughout the East, in the existence of hidden treasures, and that Europeans possess the knowledge of discovering them, renders the inhabitants exceedingly jealous of our exploring ancient ruins, as they cannot comprehend any other object we can have in the pursuit than that of wishing to carry off these secret stores of wealth. Some also entertain a conviction, that there are magic qualities existing in ancient relics, which we have the power of converting to use; and the high price we frequently give for objects of this description serves to countenance their opinion.

May 13.—We had a curious proof this morning of the respect in which the English character is held in this country. Mr. Lamb, wishing to draw a bill upon Bagdad for the sum of one hundred tomauns, for our common expenditure, sent a servant into the town to know whether any of the shraufs (merchants) would be willing to give him money for it. After a short time, a miserable half-starved looking wretch made his appearance, and said he should be willing to advance us any sum we might require: at first we were inclined to laugh at his proposal, thinking, from his appearance and garb, that he was more like an object of charity than a lender of money. He soon undeceived us; for disencumbering himself of a few of his rags, he unstrapped from his body a black leathern belt, and having cut it open, counted out the hundred tomauns in gold. Mr. Lamb wrote a draft, in English, upon a merchant in Bagdad, which this man took in lieu of his money, contenting himself with merely asking the name of the merchant on whom the bill was drawn, and declaring himself to be the party obliged; "for," said he, "if I am robbed, I shall at least be spared this piece of paper." While we were wondering both at his ability to serve us, and his confidence in our honesty (for we could easily have deceived him), he said he had had too many proofs of English probity to entertain any alarm on that head. "The *Feringhees* (Franks) are not so worthy of being trusted, but the *Ingreez* (Englishmen) have never been known to deceive."

This circumstance reflects not a little on the general good conduct of our countrymen in Persia; for in this, as well as in many other examples, it might be shown that it is to Englishmen only that this confidence is extended. Of the *Feringhees*, as it is their custom to distinguish other Europeans from us the *Ingreez*, they are as distrustful as they are of each other. Why we should have so excellent a character, I know not, though I have heard it somewhat oddly accounted for. It is said, that some time ago, an American vessel, in a trading voyage up the Red Sea, bought a considerable quantity of coffee, and paid for it in Spanish dollars, but the ship had not long sailed, when it was discovered that the money was counterfeit, and the merchants, in their indignation, vowed they would have no dealings with the English, for (as these sailors spoke our language) such they supposed them to be. Some one said that they were not English, but *Feringhee dooneaine noo*, "Franks of the New World," by which name the Americans are designated in these countries. As the mart where this transaction occurred, was on the road to Mecca, the story rapidly spread, and numerous pilgrims, on their return home, were of course glad to promulgate any story detrimental to the Christian character. It is not to be supposed that our countrymen are always immaculate; but now, if an Englishman misbehaves, he is not designated a native of England, but a "Frank of the New World." This is rather hard upon Brother Jonathan, who is to the full as honest as John Bull; but, as in many other cases, the roguery of an individual is oftentimes felt by a multitude.

I have, in a preceding page, brought a Chupper or mounted messenger to notice. I now beg to introduce this money-changer, Ishmael by name, as a Cassid, or foot messenger, showing the other channel through which the inhabitants of one city communicate with another. Ishmael was at this time on his way from Teheraun to Bagdad, having business to transact at Hamadan and Kermanshah, with probably nearly all the merchants of these cities.

CHAPTER V.

Departure for Teheraun—The Prince's arrival prevented by the Astrologers—The March of Alexander—Our Persian Costume—Advice to Travellers—Beebee Rubaut—Fatiguing March to Kujur Minar—Plain of Rubaut—Rubaut Kereem—Bukhtiari Banditti—Arrival at Teheraun—Persian Bath—Dyeing beards—Nigauristoon—Persian Flowers—Rhages—Visit Meerza Abool Hassan Khan—Kissera Kajar—Levee of the Ameen ed Dowlah—The Palace—Court Dress—The Prince Governor of Teheraun—Presentation to the King—Bastinado.

Mr. Hamilton and myself had been waiting for some days past for a *rukum*, before we commenced our march to Teheraun; but the vizier informed us that it could not be granted till the return of Tamas Meerza, as his royal signet was necessary to the document. The Prince's arrival had been daily expected, and our patience was nearly exhausted, when we heard that his Highness had been on the eve of setting out for Hamadan, but had been prevented by the astrologers telling him that some misfortune would befall him, if he returned to his capital till after the Ramazan. This intelligence decided our movements. Being too much pressed for time to be influenced by the stars, we set out at an early hour this morning for the capital.

According to Arrian, Alexander the Great, having failed in overtaking Darius at Ecbatana, continued the pursuit to Rhagæ, at which city, after many difficulties, he arrived on the eleventh day. If, as is generally believed, Hamadan is the site of Ecbatana, we must have pursued the same, or a parallel route with Alexander ; as the ruins of Rhagæ are only three miles distant from Teheraun.

Having now had some experience in the Eastern mode of travelling, and expedition being the order of the day, we disburdened ourselves of every superfluous article, and sallied forth, equipped in light marching order.

Leaving our tents behind us, and our heavy baggage with our friends, who were to travel more at their leisure to Tabriz, we reserved to ourselves six changes of linen, and our full uniforms. Instead of a number of mules, which had always occupied an hour on every day's journey in the lading, we had each our own two horses, one for riding, and the other for baggage, on the top of which a servant rode.

Up to this time we had always appeared in the honourable garb of British soldiers, of which we were sufficiently proud not to wish a change; but, to avoid a recurrence of such an adventure as that at Concobar, we thought it expedient to adopt the Persian dress: not as a disguise, but because we thought that it was not so much to ourselves as Europeans, as to the singularity of our costume, that the impertinence and importunity of the mob had been generally directed.

The British officers at Tabriz advise travellers to wear the English dress. It is certainly best for the direct road through Persia, where it is known and respected; but the dress of the country is strongly recommended to any one pursuing our less frequented route.

Our head-dress was a black sheep-skin cap, pinched into a peak behind, and fitting the head rather closely before. A pale blue gown, which extended to the calf of the leg, was neatly crimped, and decorated with innumerable little sugar-loaf buttons down each side of the chest, and from the elbow to the wrist. This gown was open in many parts, and discovered beneath it, what I fear must be called a petticoat, ornamented with a pine-apple pattern on a bright purple ground; over this was bound loosely round the waist a scarlet shawl. A capacious pair of silk trowsers, of a pale pink, covered the lower extremities. It is hoped that scarlet Hessian boots, in size equal to those in which Hogarth has drawn Hudibras, sabres by our sides, our pistols and dagger in our girdles, and our formidable mustaches, will in some degree redeem the effeminacy of our garb.

After quitting the town we traversed the fertile valley of Hamadan, and passed over a low mountain, on the brow of which wild flowers of every hue combined their fragrance with innumerable aromatic shrubs. We then came into a spacious plain, and followed the most beaten track till the road diverged into several branches. Being without a guide, we took the path which appeared to lead to a large town. Here we thought we could distinctly see the trees, the domes of the mosques, and the bastions of the walls; but after proceeding in the same direction for nearly three miles, it vanished, and we now discovered that we had been led astray by that curious optical delusion so common in the East, called the Saharaub, literally, "water of the desert." We were the more surprised at being deceived by this phenomenon, as from the day we landed we had been daily witnesses to its curious properties.

At one in the afternoon, we arrived at Beebee Rubaut, a small untenanted village. We had intended, after a few hours' rest, to have proceeded onwards, but were dissuaded by one of the King's Shatirs (footmen), who with three other servants were proceeding to

Teheraun the next day. As not one of our party had ever been this road, which was described as very intricate, we put ourselves under the convoy of these men, and agreed to accompany them the next morning.

May 15.—This stage, which could not have been less than sixty miles, was the most painful, and the least interesting, we had yet made. We commenced our march at the rising, and finished it at the setting of the sun, having had the full benefit of its scorching rays, which became every moment more intense as the snow-capped mountains of Hamadan receded from our view. Our road lay either through sterile and desolate mountains, or stony valleys formed by the beds of torrents. With the exception of a miserable village twelve miles from Beebee Rubaut, where we breakfasted, we did not see a single building: not a traveller passed to diversify the dull uniformity of the scene; and we reached Kujur Minar, our destination, so dispirited and feverish, that though our lodging was good, and our dinner tolerable, we could scarcely eat or sleep.

May 16.—After a few hours of imperfect rest, we started at three in the morning for the village of Chummurum, distant twenty miles. For the first six hours we traversed a country of the same appearance as that of yesterday: at nine we crossed a fordable river, which divides the districts of Hamadan and Teheraun, and entered upon a fruitful and well cultivated valley, the banks of the stream being strongly contrasted with that we had just quitted. Except in spots where extensive crops were growing, the whole valley looked like one vast meadow. There was also an appearance of extensive population, as numerous villages seemed to deck the plain: but this in Persia is an "optical delusion," as common as the Saharaub; for on our nearer approach we found they were the ruins of deserted villages.

Leaning our backs against one of the walls, as a protection against the heat of the sun, we made a hasty breakfast, and, resuming our march, reached Chummurum at mid-day.

May 17.—At three A. M. we started for Zerun, a long march of fifty-two miles. The morning was very dark; and after wandering an hour, we had the bad fortune to lose our way: chance directed us to a village, where we procured a guide, and were led through a narrow pass of the mountains into the direct road.

The pasture with which these wild mountains are somewhat sparingly covered, afforded subsistence to numbers of the King's camels, on the ungraceful forms of which, in the absence of all other living creatures, we gazed with satisfaction.

We continued winding through successive

ranges of hills till we came on to the spacious plain of Rubaut. It appears to be about forty miles in length, and twelve or fourteen in breadth. Hence we could discern the mountains immediately behind Teheraun.

Half way across this plain stood the village of Zerun, where a small narrow apartment was allotted for our accommodation. On the ceiling of our new dwelling was a circular hole, which, though intended only for the admission of light and air, did not exempt rain: of this we became aware in the middle of the night, being awoke by a smart shower, which, before we could make our escape, had completely drenched us to the skin.

May 18.—We resumed our march over the plain at five in the morning; and saw at some distance a small palace, to which the King goes every winter for the pleasures of the chase: here antelopes and various other kinds of game, are said to be very abundant.

We halted half an hour on the plain to enable our Persian fellow-travellers to eat their breakfast; but as no water was procurable, we deferred our own meal till we arrived at our stage: indeed, we acted thus on the whole march from Hamadan to Teheraun.

The scarcity of water here brings to mind the anecdote related by Plutarch of Alexander the Great, while on the same road:—Being one day overcome with heat and thirst, he met some Macedonians carrying water on mules in sheep-skins for their children. These men, on witnessing the exhausted appearance of the king, filled a helmet with water, and brought it to him to drink; but he, observing the eager looks with which his soldiers regarded the water, returned it to the Macedonians, and by this act so captivated his followers, that they said they were neither tired nor thirsty, and considered themselves immortal, whilst they had such a man for a king.

Four miles from Rubaut Kereem, we passed a succession of hillocks, which were pointed out to us as being much infested with banditti of the Bukhtiari tribe. We arrived at the town at one o'clock, and, being now only twenty-four miles from Teheraun, despatched a villager forward to give Major Willock notice of our arrival.

May 19.—An hour after midnight we remounted our horses, being anxious to conclude this wretched journey. Six miles from Rubaut Kereem, the Shatir pointed out to us several villages, a short distance from the road, as being entirely inhabited by Bukhtiari banditti; but we saw none of them, nor, indeed, any one else on this solitary road. The sun rose in fiery splendour over the mountains of Teheraun, but the city itself is in so low a situation, that we could not distinguish it till we were not more than two miles distant. Here we were met by Major Willock and Dr. Macneil, who, being dressed in the English fashion, made us feel ashamed of our foreign disguise. We were conducted by our countrymen to the English residency, and by their care and attentions soon lost the unpleasant recollection of our miserable march.

In the afternoon we went to the Hummaum. In addition to the usual process of an eastern bath, the barber had dyed my mustaches before I was aware of his intention. Generally speaking, there are two sorts of dye used; they are made up in the form of a paste: one is henna, the other indigo. If the hair is dark, the henna is first put on, which turns the hair quite red. When dry this is washed off, indigo is substituted, and a jet black is soon produced. As my hair was light, the indigo only was used. This being the first time of wearing a dye, the skin became slightly affected, but it soon recovered. In the course of a few hours, my mustaches, after undergoing the alarming transitions from green to purple, settled at last into a fine auburn.

We employed the ten days of our stay at Teheraun in visiting every thing remarkable in and about the city. On the 21st, Major Willock took us to see one of the King's palaces, called Nigauristoon, or Garden of Pictures. It is an oblong enclosure, containing three summer-houses. In the uppermost of these, at the top of the room, are painted on the wall fresco portraits of the King and several of his sons. His Majesty is seated on his throne, and the princes stand beside him. The sides of the apartment are decorated with the figures of all the ambassadors that have at different periods appeared at the Persian court. To these the king is (with a poetic licence) supposed to be giving audience at the same time. On one side of the wall this motley assemblage is headed by the three English ambassadors, Sir John Malcolm, Sir Gore Ouseley, and Sir Harford Jones. On the other, for the sake of uniformity, there are three French ambassadors, though only one ever came to Persia. The European portraits, as may be supposed, are complete caricatures, but in the delineation of Asiatic dresses and features, the artist has been more successful. The other summer-houses are hardly worthy of notice: though newly erected, they have the usual Persian marks of dirt and decay. A stream of water, running in a channel of masonry, supplies a jet-d'eau in the centre building. On each side of the garden are a few formal rows of poplar; behind them are some cypress and some fruit-trees. There are also a variety of shrubs, some flowers, and no scarcity of weeds. It is let by the King for two hundred tomauns a-year, to one of the courtiers; who is obliged to keep it in repair. As the tenant has no taste either for beauty or neatness, he sows that which will yield him most profit: a clover-stubble marks his last crop.

Notwithstanding their poetic admiration of flowers, the Persians treat them with much neglect; still there are many which are beautiful and well worthy of notice. I am no botanist, so I must content myself with mentioning those which attracted my attention. The most remarkable in appearance is a large rose-tree, called the Nasteraun: it grows to the height of twenty feet; the trunk is nearly two feet in circumference; the flower, though larger, resembles the English hedge-rose, and has five leaves; the calix is in the form of a bell. The leaf of the tree is small, smooth, and shining. The branches droop gracefully to the ground, and the flowers are so abundant as completely to conceal the stem of the tree. Numbers of this species are to be seen in every garden in Teheraun.

The next is the Durukhti Ubrishoom, a

species of Mimosa, resembling the Arborea of that genus. It droops like the willow; the flower has silky fibres, of a delicate pink colour, and would resemble a swansdown puff, tinged with rouge. It sends forth a most fragrant perfume, and its name, "Durukhti Ubrishoom," the Silk-tree,—bespeaks its appearance. This flower thrives in Teheraun in the open air; the thermometer ranging between 16° and 110°, Farenheit; but it does not succeed so well at Tabriz, where the temperature is colder and more variable. It grows wild in the forests bordering on the Caspian Sea. There is one in the garden of the Prince Royal at Tabriz, and another in possession of the English officers resident there, who are obliged to protect it from the winter cold.

The Zunjeed is also a species of willow. The leaves are of a silvery hue, and the flowers, which are of a deep scarlet, send forth a most delicious perfume. When in blossom, the Zunjeed is viewed with a jealous eye by the Persians, from the belief that it has a strong tendency to excite the passions of the females. The Persian who was describing the curious properties of this tree, told me that twelve fursungs north of Teheraun, the men lock up their women while the flower is in blow.

May 22.—Five miles south of Teheraun are the ruins of the ancient City of Rhages, mentioned in the book of Tobit, as also by Arrian and Diodorus Siculus. To this city Alexander came in pursuit of the unfortunate Darius, and halted here five days previous to his expedition into Parthia.

Rhages continued to flourish till the time of Jenghiz Khan, whose general destroyed it, and Teheraun, the modern capital, arose from out of its ruins. It has met with the usual fate of old brick buildings; it has crumbled into dust, and a few shapeless heaps are nearly all the memorials of this once populous city. I should except a well-built tower, which I had not time to examine, and the commencement of a bas-relief cut in the rock, representing two warriors in the act of combat.

May 23.—We accompanied Major Willock this morning on a visit to Meerza Abool Hassan Khan, the late Persian Ambassador to the English Court. This gentleman is more portly than he was in London, and may be said to have grown fat on the pension which the India Company has granted him—for what services the Meerza probably knows as little as any one else; for, if common report be true, there are few men more hostile to our interests than himself. Notwithstanding all this, he is a very agreeable companion, and received us with much politeness.

After smoking a pipe in the common hall of audience, the Meerza conducted us into one of the rooms of his haram. The women had been previously warned to withdraw themselves; but whether by accident or from design, one or two lingered so long that we had a good view of their faces. They wore large turbans, and one of them seemed a pretty girl. The room we now entered partook of the European and Asiatic styles. The walls were hung with prints, which, for the honour of my own country, I am glad to say were not English. If the Meerza speak true, he has not been unsuccessful with the English ladies; if not, their civilities to him have been shamefully misinterpreted.

Our next visit was to the Kissera Kajar, the Palace of the Kajar or Royal Tribe of Persia. It stands two miles north-east of the town. When viewed from a distance, it has the appearance of a building several stories high; on approaching nearer, it proves to be a succession of terraces, built on the slope of a mountain. It is intended for a summer retreat, and is traversed in all directions by streams of water, which render it cool and pleasant. On the fifth terrace, we enter upon the principal part of the building: here are several pictures, some representing the ancient Kings of Persia, and all executed in a style greatly superior to any other specimens of the art I saw in this country. On the summit of the palace is a small but beautiful chamber; the windows and doors are inlaid with ebony and ivory, describing Persian characters: there are also several fine samples of Mosaic work, and some curious enamel paintings. The female apartments comprise a succession of small chambers, twelve or fourteen feet square: in each of these is a high wooden bedstead, occupying nearly the whole space, and said to contain a family: if so, the ladies of the royal haram must be stowed almost as close as negroes on board a slave-ship. The walls are whitewashed, but in a dirty state:

they are without decoration, if I except the poetical effusions of their fair inmates, whose writings may be traced in every apartment.

At ten at night, Major Willock, Dr. Macneil, Meerza Abool Hassan Khan, Mr. Hamilton, and myself, attended the public levee of the Ameen ed Dowlah, Lord Treasurer, who performed the duties of Prince Vizier, that office being vacant. The reception-room was spacious and unadorned. The minister, who was seated in a corner, rose to bid us welcome; a compliment he does not pay to his own countrymen. The visitors all sate with their backs to the wall: four or five thick candles in low tin candlesticks stood in the middle of the room: several Meerzas (Secretaries) were seated in a semicircle opposite the minister, and upon papers held in the palm of the left hand were writing from his dictation. The company in general had no particular business; those who had, went up by turns to the minister, made their statement in a whisper, and retired with a low bow. Servants came in at intervals with culaoons, which were rapidly passed from mouth to mouth. Every person in this assembly sate according to his rank. On our arriving, a place was immediately given to us near the minister: in other parts of the room such a concession was not so willingly made, and an amusing struggle for precedence ensued at the arrival of every new comer, who was excluded from a seat till the humility or good-humour of some one made room for him. As soon as we had settled the object of our visit,—a presentation to the King, which was fixed for twelve o'clock on the day after, we made our bows to the minister and retired.

May 26.—At twelve o'clock we accompanied Major Willock to the palace; but by mistake his Majesty was not apprised of our arrival till it was too late; so he sent a message to desire our attendance at four in the afternoon. We saw here several courtiers retiring from the daily levee, at which the King, whether in sickness or in health, is obliged to be present,—one of the taxes levied upon despotic power.

The court-dress is simple, but rich; the common sheep-skin cap is covered with a superb Cachemire shawl. Over the homely cotton gown, ordinarily worn by all ranks, is a scarlet cloth robe: a pair of boots of the same materials completes the costume.

We spent an hour in examining the palace. The outward gate opens into a spacious court-yard, in which are several cannons of various dimensions. In the centre is a large gun, which was taken from Lootf Ali Khan, the last Persian king of the Zund family. Over each of the four gateways is a large drawing formed of glazed tiles, and executed in a truly grotesque manner. In one of these, Rustam, the Persian Hercules, is engaged in fierce contest with the Deevee Safeed, the celebrated White Demon of Ferdousi's poem.

This court leads to a second. In the centre of this is a piece of water surrounded by poplars. The Dewan Khoneh is at the further end. In this chamber is a large marble throne, on which his Majesty sits on extraordinary occasions. The walls and wainscoting are of the finest mosaic. There is a great profusion of ornamental glass of all colours, describing flowers. The ceiling of this room is a succession of looking-glasses divided by flowered ornaments. In every recess or panel there is some picture: in one is a hunting piece, in another a battle, in others portraits of the King. I was much amused at the style of some of the smaller paintings. One professes to represent Nadir Shah returning the crown to the Indian king, after having wrested it from him; the right hand of Nadir grasps the club of state, the left rests on the crown; but so fierce is the expression of the conqueror, and so peculiar his attitude, that it seems as if he intended to knock down the Indian monarch. A second exhibits Noorsheer-van giving audience to the Grand Signior, the artist forgetting that the Persian monarch, having died before Mahomet, could not have been a contemporary with one of his successors. In a third picture we have Iskunder (Alexander the Great) listening to the discourse of Ufflatoon and Aristo (Plato and Aristotle). The Macedonian hero is dressed in the modern Persian fashion, and the two great philosophers are habited like common dervishes.

In the course of the morning we paid our respects to Ali Khan Meerza, a favourite son of the king's, governor of Teheraun, and designated by the title of Zilli Sultan, (Shadow of the Sultan,) as the king is called Zil Illah, (the Shadow of God). This prince is born of the same mother as Abbas Meerza, with whom it is thought, after the death of the King, he will have a contest for the crown. His Highness is very handsome, and very vain. We made a profound bow on entering, and were graciously invited to sit down, an honour granted to no Persians except princes of the blood. Five of these were present at our visit. One, a boy about ten years old, was dressed in a gown of light blue cloth richly embroidered, and was the handsomest lad I ever saw. In fact, the present royal tribe of Persia is unrivalled in personal beauty. Ali Khan Meerza had several trinkets by him—a string of beads, and a small crutch to support him in a sitting posture; but what seemed to give him most satisfaction was a hand mirror, at which, ever and anon, he gazed with much complacency.

At the appointed hour, Meerza Abool Hassan Khan, Major Willock, Mr. Hamilton, and myself, set out for our interview with his Majesty. The Persian was in his court-dress, we were in full uniform; and we all wore green slippers, and the court boots of red cloth, without which no one can approach His Majesty.

The King received us in a small palace in the middle of a garden, called the Gulestan —Rose Garden. When arrived at the top of the avenue which led to it, we imitated the motions of the Meerza, and bowed several times, our hands touching our knees at each reverence. We had, at this time, a good side-view of the King, who, apparently from established etiquette, took no notice of us. We repeated our bows at intervals. When within twenty yards of the palace, we left our slippers behind us, and the King, turning towards us for the first time, called out, "Bee-au-bala"—Ascend. A narrow flight of steps brought us to the presence-chamber. It is an elegant apartment, open at two opposite sides, where it is supported by spiral pillars painted white and red; a large carpet is spread on the floor; the walls and ceiling are completely covered with looking-glass. One or two European clocks stand in different parts of the room; but the accumulation of dust upon them shows that they are considered useless lumber.

On entering this chamber, we walked sideways to the most remote corner from that which the King occupied. After the usual compliments of welcome, His Majesty asked several questions respecting our journey, and surprised us not a little at his geographical knowledge, both with regard to the country we had quitted, and that which we purposed to visit. The audience lasted twenty minutes; his Majesty was in high good-humour, and conversed with unaffected ease on a variety of subjects. The titles used at the interview were "Kubla-hi-Aulim and Shah-in-Shahi"—Attraction of the World, and King of Kings. He was seated on his heels on some doubled nummuds, the Persians priding themselves on this hard seat, in contradistinction to their enemies the Turks, whom they charge with effeminacy for their use of cushions.

The King had a variety of toys, which gave employment to his hands, and assisted his gestures in conversation. One of these trinkets was a Chinese ivory hand at the end of a thin stick, called by us in India a scratch-back, a name which faithfully denotes its office: another was a crutch, three feet long, the shaft of ebony, and the head of crystal. His Majesty has the appearance of a younger man than he really is, but his voice, which is hollow from the loss of teeth, is a better indication of his age. I should have known him from his strong resemblance to the prints I had seen of him in London. I think, however, they hardly do justice to his beard, which is so large that it conceals all the face but the forehead and eyes, and extends down to the girdle. He was very plainly dressed, wearing a cotton gown of a dark colour, and the common sheep-skin cap. In his girdle was a dagger, superbly studded with jewels of an extraordinary size.

The dress of the modern Persian has undergone so complete a change, that much resemblance to the ancient costume is not to be expected; still there are some marks of decoration, which remind one of the ancient monarchs. The eyelids of the king, stained with surmeh, brought to our recollection the surprise of the young and hardy Cyrus, when he viewed for the first time a similar embellishment in his effeminate uncle, Astyages; and in that extraordinary chapter of Ezekiel, wherein Jerusalem is reproached for her imitation of Babylonian manners, the prophet alludes to this custom, when he says, "Thou paintedst thine eyes." *

A bracelet, consisting of a ruby and

* Ez. xxiii. 40.

emerald, worn by the king on his arm, is a mark of ancient sovereignty. It will be recollected that the Amalekites brought David the bracelet found on Saul's arm, as a proof of his rank; and Herodotus mentions a bracelet of gold as a present from Cambyses, King of Persia, to the King of Ethiopia.

I must not omit the mention of a circumstance connected with our interview, as it illustrates a piece of etiquette at the court of a despotic monarch. A few minutes before we were presented, we observed two men carrying a long pole and a bundle of sticks towards the audience chamber. Curiosity led us to ask the Meerza what was the meaning of this. "That machine," said he, "is the bastinado; it is for you, if you misbehave. Those men are carrying it to the King, who never grants a private audience without having it by him, in case of accidents." The pole we saw was about eight feet long: when the punishment is inflicted, the culprit is thrown on his back, his feet are secured by cords bound round the ankles, and made fast to the pole with the soles uppermost; the pole is held by a man at both ends, and two men, one on each side, armed with sticks, strike with such force that the toe-nails frequently drop off. This punishment is inflicted by order of the King upon men of the highest rank, generally for the purpose of extorting money. If Persia was not so fond of illustrating the use of this emblem of power, she would have as much right to the "Bastinado," as we have to the "Black Rod."

CHAPTER VI.

Summer Palace of Ali Khan Meerza—Gypsies—Soolimanea, Sougherabad, and Sufur Khojah—Casbin—Serah Dahn—Aubhaur—Saingula—Curious Animals—Ruins of Sultanieh—Tomb of Sultan Khodabundah—King's Summer Palace—Zingaun—Town, Bazaar, Mosque—Armaghanah—Auk-kend—Kaufilan Koh—Mountain of Tigers—Kizil Oozan—Bridge—Rude Scenery—Murder of Mr. Brown—Superstitions—Kurz Kula—Causeway—Oppression of Drowsiness—Arrive at Mæana—Curious Exhibition—Description of Mæana—Extraordinary Bug and Earth Louse—Turcoman Sha-ee—Tikhmadash—Wasmitch—Arrival at Tabriz—Departure of Messrs. Lamb and Hart—Introduction to the Prince Royal.

May 27.—We made an excursion of ten miles to the Demawund Mountains, and stopped to breakfast at a summer palace of Ali Khan Meerza, a true picture of a Persian residence, whether belonging to prince or peasant—dirty chambers, broken windows, and dilapidated walls. In the garden which surrounded it, weeds had usurped the place of flowers. Luckily for us the nightingales did not sympathize with the proprietor's neglect, but warbled delightfully during our repast.

Close to this place was an encampment of gypsies. They are called in Persian, Girauchee. There is nothing to distinguish them from the other wandering tribes, who, it is said, hold them in low estimation.

The valley at the base of this mountain is called Shuma Iroon, the Light of Persia. It is celebrated for the salubrity of the air, and the beauty of its situation. It is richly wooded. The numerous pleasure-houses, mosques, and villages peeping from out the branches, form a pleasing contrast to the various shades of the verdant foliage. A large waterfall rushes down the rock, and breaking into several channels, traverses the habitations, and fertilizes the plain below.

May 28.—One of my horses dying, I obtained an order for three of the King's post-horses. We started from Teheraun in the evening, and arrived at a caravanserai in the course of the night.

May 29—30.—*June* 1.—Nothing worthy of notice occurred in the first three days of our march. Soolimanea, our first stage, was twenty-four miles, Sougherabad twelve, and Sufur Khojah thirty. The country throughout is intersected by channels for irrigation, the land is well cultivated, and the harvest abundant. The population here is greater than in any place we have yet seen in Persia.

June 2.—On the morning of the 2nd, we came to Casbin, the seat of a Prince Governor. Our first quarters were in a stable, where we were nearly driven mad by the musquitos; but the King's order soon procured us an apartment in the palace.

This city, once the capital of the kingdom, is still sufficiently populous to carry on an extensive trade with Ghilaun, but it is a Persian town, and therefore in ruins. Some remains of the buildings of the Abbacidæ may yet be seen. The gardens of Casbin produce abundance of fruit, and the grapes of the surrounding vineyards are unequalled in Persia.

At ten at night I obtained an interview of the Prince. He was seated in the veranda of a circular summer-house, situate in a pretty garden. Aided by the bright light of an Eastern moon, I could almost fancy this residence a fairy habitation. It was hung round with Chinese lanterns, the variegated light of which was reflected on the group of surrounding courtiers, and tinged with a silvery hue the neighbouring fountain. This was the outline—imagination filled up the picture.

I did not stipulate for my privilege as an

Englishman, to be seated in the Prince's presence, fearing that, if I did, I should not obtain an interview; so I was obliged to stand before him. I was presented by his Mehmaundaur, whose motions of reverence I imitated. His Highness's manner was haughty, but it seemed habitual and not assumed. He asked me several questions, mostly respecting himself: to these I always tried to give a reasonable answer; but the Mehmaundaur, pretending to attribute my plainness of language to ignorance of idiom, turned every thing I said into an extravagant compliment to the Prince, and then asked me if that was not what I intended to say. To dissent was impossible; so I let him have his own way, and thus all parties were pleased.

June 3.—We reached Serah Dahn, a march of twenty-two miles, in seven hours. The village is small, but surrounded by extensive fields of corn ready for the sickle.

June 4.—From Serah Dahn to Aubhaur,

thirty-one miles, was an uninteresting march, over a succession of low hills. Aubhaur stands in the midst of a clump of trees, and is surrounded by a well-cultivated tract of land. The Persians assign it a high antiquity. As we devoted the few hours of our stay to rest, we did not ascertain whether there were any ancient ruins. From the coincidences in the sound of the name, and from the geographical relation of the place to others, it is supposed to be "Habor, by the river Gozan," where Hoshea, King of Assyria, carried Israel away captive. The Kizzel Ozan, the reputed Gozan of Scripture, which we crossed three days afterwards, is forty-five miles from Aubhaur.

June 5.—We left our quarters before dusk, marched sixteen miles, and halted for a few hours at the village of Saingula; we then proceeded to Sultanieh, eighteen miles distant.

We passed over a plain swarming with animals resembling rats, which live in burrows, and are so tame that they will hardly get out of the way of the passing traveller.

June 6.—In the middle of the plain is Sultanieh, a city founded six hundred years ago by Sultan Khodabundah, but now completely in ruins. Amidst the heaps of fallen houses, the only building worthy of notice is the tomb of the founder. It is a noble structure, consisting of a beautifully shaped cupola on an octangular base, and is a hundred feet high. The outside has been covered with a sort of glazed tile, observable in many old Eastern buildings. In the interior are the remains of some fine Arabesque workmanship; but time, aided by the more active operations of destructive man, has made it difficult to trace the original beauties. There are several Arabic and Cufic inscriptions painted in fresco on the walls, but these are daily becoming more obliterated, as workmen are taking away the materials of the tomb for other buildings.

The King comes to Sultanieh every summer, to avoid the heat of Teheraun. When we left the capital, His Majesty was to set out in a fortnight.

We visited the palace this afternoon; the ascent to it is up a steep and narrow staircase. It is a mean and ill-built dwelling, and the rooms are extremely filthy. The doorway of one of the apartments was bricked up, but opened to allow us to enter. This is a private apartment of the King's. At the bottom of the room, is a farcical representation of his Majesty on horseback, in the act of spearing a wild ass. In all the panels are full-length fresco portraits of different sons of the King. The Dewan Khoneh, or hall of audience, leads on to a terrace. The King sits in the most elevated part; a little below is a place for the Princes and nobles; and another, lower still, for the inferior classes. The plain of Sultanieh cannot boast a single tree; we saw no birds, and, instead of the melody of nightingales, we heard only the croaking of frogs.

June 7.—On arriving at Zinjaun, a journey of twenty-six miles, we heard that Messrs. Lamb and Hart had passed through a few days before; that they had been overtaken by a violent thunder-storm, and that some of their baggage-mules had been carried away by the mountain torrent.

Zinjaun is the capital of the district of Khumseh, and is governed by Abdoolah Meerza one of the King's sons, who resides here. The town is large and populous; it is enclosed in a mud wall, in good repair. The bazaar is superior to those at Hamadan and Kermanshah, and almost equal to that at Bagdad. It extends from the eastern to the western gate, and is covered over the whole way with light thatch. The shops are well stored with all the usual articles of consumption. A new bazaar, not yet finished, branches off into the great one, and terminates in the square in front of the palace. One portion is finished, and the shops are occupied; the other part is incomplete, and apparently going to ruin. It is vaulted throughout, and upon the whole is well built. Adjoining the bazaar, and fronting the palace, a superb mosque is erecting; the front is covered with enamelled bricks in the form of Mosaic. It is complete to the first story; and the principal arch, which is formed of hewn stone, has a solid and handsome appearance. The Mehmaun Khoneh is situate close to the eastern gate, in a fortified suburb.

June 8.—We passed along the outside of the city wall to the south; we then entered on a stony plain, thinly covered with verdure. Our road followed the direction of a river to the N. W., along a hollow bounded on each side by high banks, which the stream has excavated in the course of ages. This hollow, formed of rich alluvial soil, is well cultivated, and covered with luxuriant crops of wheat. The country throughout is populous and cultivated. A fursukh from Zinjaun, we passed a large village on the banks of a river, with extensive gardens and groves of trees. Several other villages, surrounded by gardens, were visible, both on the banks of the stream and in the hollows of mountains, which bound the valley on both sides. In a march of twenty-four miles we reached the small town of Armaghanah, in the bosom of a verdant valley.

June 9.—Our next day's journey was to Auk-kend, a distance of twenty-eight miles, over a hilly uninteresting country.

The following night at nine we set out for Mæanah. We continued traversing hills till we arrived at the range of mountains called Kaufilan Koh, Mountain of Tigers. At the top of this range we first saw the Kizil Oozan, the Golden Stream.

The moon, which had been shining brightly,

became at length partially obscured by a cloud, and showed to effect the bold outline of these black and craggy mountains, and at the same time reflecting on the river beneath, gave it the appearance of some vast shining serpent creeping through the dark and lonesome valley. According to Rennell, the Kizil Oozan is the Gozan of Scripture. We crossed it at one in the morning, over a handsome brick bridge; and by so doing quitted Irak, and entered upon the district of Azerbijan, the government of Abbas Meerza, the Prince Royal of Persia.

In former times, Azerbijan was called Atropatena, from the Satrap Atropates, who, after the death of Alexander, assumed the title of King of this country, and transmitted it to his posterity, who retained it for several generations.

The structure of this bridge, as far as we could judge, indicates both skill and taste in the architect. It consists of three large arches, the centre the largest: the arches are lofty, to allow a passage for the water at the highest floods: the piers, which are very massy at the base, are relieved from the spring of the arches by a smaller arch, which gives a lightness of appearance and diminishes the pressure. Part of the sides are fallen in, and the bridge itself stands a fair chance of soon becoming impassable, when the communication of this road will be stopped for many months in the year. The scenery here is exceedingly wild. Immediately below the bridge, the river passes by a narrow channel between lofty precipitous mountains, that rise almost perpendicular in rude rugged masses. By the bright light of the moon, we saw down the river, at a little distance from the bridge, and at a considerable elevation, the remains of an ancient fort, standing on a detached rock of an irregular form. This rises nearly perpendicular on all sides, and is said to be the haunt of robbers,

Our Mehmaundaur spoke of the danger of travelling here without an officer appointed by the King. It was not far hence that Mr. Brown, the African traveller, was murdered, whose misfortune may be attributed to his not taking with him a Mehmaundaur.

Numerous tales are current regarding this desolate spot. It is said to be the scene of many extraordinary occurrences, both of an earthly and supernatural kind. Remote from human habitation, this is not surprising in a country where robbers are plenty, and superstition prevalent. The fort is called Kurz Kula, Daughter's Fort, said to have been built by the daughter of a king, but at what time is unknown: the bridge has probably been erected at the same time.

Crossing the bridge, we commenced the ascent of a steep mountain, which took us an hour. About half way up, we saw the remains of a causeway, which, we were told, can be traced to the top. It appears to have been continued throughout the whole extent of the mountain. In some parts it is entire. The descent on the opposite side, towards Mæana, is very steep. Mr. Hamilton and myself suffered much from the intense oppression of drowsiness: to complete the matter, my horse was seized with the gripes, and continued every half mile to lie down with me in the midst of the precipitous declivity. This sensation of wanting to sleep on a march is the most distressing inconvenience of an over-land journey.

We were nearly two hours in reaching the bottom. Beyond this is an open plain of considerable extent. About a mile from the foot of the mountain, we crossed a river, running to the S. W., by a flat bridge of twenty-three equal arches, two miles beyond Mæana.

June 10.—On entering the town we were witnesses to rather a curious exhibition. I should first mention that the Persians are in the habit of sleeping on the flat roofs of their houses during the summer months. Day was just breaking when we arrived. As the houses of the poorer classes are generally not more than eight feet high, we had a full view of nearly the whole population in bed. Many were asleep; some few had awoke; others were getting out of bed, to make their morning toilette. The scene was highly entertaining, and brought to mind the story of Le Diable Boiteux unroofing the houses for the gratification of Don Cleofas.

Mæana stands on the site of the Atropatena of ancient history, the capital of Atropatia, the modern Azerbijan. Both town and district derived their names from Atropates. It is situate on a low swampy plain. Though half in ruins, it is still large and populous. It has numerous gardens, and is extensively cultivated. A large palace and garden, belonging to the Prince Royal, stand only a few hundred yards from the town; a situation in which one would scarcely expect to find a royal residence. We saw the remains of an ancient building, apparently the wall of a fort, built of large hewn stones regularly squared, but we could not learn any thing respecting it. Mæana is celebrated for the manufacture of carpets. It is said to be the head-quarters of a savage tribe called Chedaughee.

We were regaled here with a story of an extraordinary bug called a mullah, a native of Mæana. This inhospitable insect, the bite of which is mortal, is said to leave the natives unmolested, and only to attack the stranger. It inhabits the crevices of old walls. If a light is burning, it comes not forth, but when all is dark, this midnight assassin stalks from its concealment, and slays the way-worn traveller.

This story, absurd as it is, has gained credit with more than one person. For ourselves, we are inclined to acquit the mullah of murderous habits, and are at least grateful to it for letting us live to tell the tale.

We cannot so easily absolve from blame another species of insect, which accompanied us from Mæana to Tabriz. It is of a diamond shape, small, white and flat. The bite produces an intolerable itching. At first, we could not imagine what caused our uneasiness, but on examining our clothes we found this animal. We observed that, after having feasted on us for a little while, a black mark appeared down its back. We understand this insect is generated in the earth, and is of the same description as the louse mentioned in Scripture as one of the plagues of Egypt; though it agrees in description with the common body-louse of our own country.

June 11.—We left Mæana in the night, travelled twenty-one miles over a hilly country, and arrived in the morning at the village of Turcoman Sha-ee, the neighbourhood of which is in a good state of cultivation.

June 12.—The next day's march was to Tikhmadash, twenty-four miles, road N. W. and hilly as usual. We passed two caravanserais in ruins, and saw several villages. In the latter part of the stage, the country was well cultivated.

Tikhmadash is a considerable village, on the brow of an eminence a mile to the west of the road. The situation is very much exposed.

June 13.—We next came to the village of Wasmitch; a laborious journey, though the distance was not more than twenty-six miles. In two hours we passed the village of Oojoon. After crossing a low bottom of marshy ground, we saw a number of oblong tomb-stones, about six feet long, and two wide and thick. The country was hilly, and presented the usual defect of Persian scenery—a total absence of wood.

This remark is applicable to almost every day's march since we left Bussorah. Once or twice in our route we might fall in with a few trees, but they were always scrupulously noted down as objects of curiosity. In towns, and in their immediate neighbourhood, there was generally a small collection, but these were mostly poplars, and rather added to the naked appearance of the country.

June 14.—We set out at daylight. Wasmitch being only nine miles from Tabriz, we had written to inform the English residents of our approach, but by the delay of our messenger the note arrived almost at the same time with us. We met Major Monteith, at the entrance of the town, riding full gallop to meet us, it being a customary compliment for the English residents in Persia to receive the strangers at the gates, and to accompany them into the town.

We were highly gratified at sitting down

to an excellent breakfast with a party of our own countrymen: after which, Mr. Hamilton became the guest of Dr. Cormick, and I of Major Monteith. The English residents at Tabriz are, Major Monteith, who is employed by the India Government in a survey of Georgia; Captain Hart, the commander of the Prince's guard; and Dr. Cormick, physician to his Royal Highness. There were besides, Major Walker and Mr. Edward Bootle Wilbraham, travellers from England; and our friends Messrs. Lamb and Hart, whom we were delighted to meet again. They had arrived at Tabriz six days before us, and being anxious to proceed to England with all possible dispatch, had intended to set out the same evening. In consequence of our arrival, they were kind enough to defer their journey till the following day.

June 15.—The next day we took our farewell dinner with Messrs. Hart and Lamb, who started at ten at night. They were accompanied by all the English outside the walls of the town. As they expected to be in England six weeks before me, I sent letters by them to my friends.

June 16.—The following morning Major Walker, Mr. Hamilton, and myself, were presented to the Abbas Meerza, the Prince Royal, by Dr. Cormick. We were received in the Dewan Khoneh, and were seated opposite the Prince. His Royal Highness addressed us with the greatest civility and kindness. In the room was a picture representing one of his successful expeditions against the Turks. This naturally introduced the subject of his wars, on which we of course made some common compliments. His Royal Highness disclaimed all credit to himself, attributing his victories entirely to the assistance of our countrymen.

I was surprised to find that his Royal Highness immediately recognized the Waterloo medal which I wore, asking me if it had not been given for having been present at the last decisive battle the English fought with Napoleon. A reply in the affirmative produced numerous civil speeches relative to that event, and the compliments we had given were repaid with interest.

Among the expressions of civility used by his Royal Highness, was "*Be-dillum, nuzdeek mee-aeed,*" "You approach near to my heart;" which phrase he continually repeated till we took our leave.

CHAPTER VII.

Dinner with Colonel Mazerowitch—Projected Route—Arrangements for the Journey—Departure from Tabriz—Appearance of the Country—Shehruk—Golijah—Aher—New Mehmaundaur—Hoja Kishlaukh—Arabshehr—Beautiful Scenery—Yokhari Perasewaun—Gulakundee—Wheat Harvest—Venomous Serpent—Illustration of Plutarch—Cross the Araxes—Illyaut Encampment—Arrival in Russian Territory—Meralian—Karabaugh, the country of the Sacaseni—Peerhumud—Luxuriant Foliage—Cossacks Haymaking—Khanakhi—Armenian Villages—Arrival at Sheesha—Appearance of the Town—Russian Officers' Quarters—Aga Beg, Chief of the Armenians, and his Brothers—Two Missionaries—Visit to the Commandant—Tomb of Nartuck—Sheesha, its Population, Trade, Climate, and Costume—Prescribe for my Host's Brother—My fame as a Physician.

WE one day dined with Colonel Mazerowitch, the Russian Chargé-d'affaires. Though all the party were Christians, and did not exceed twenty, there were present, natives of France, Spain, Italy, Germany, Holland, Russia, England, Greece, Sclavonia, Armenia, Georgia, Arabia, and Persia. Amongst the servants in attendance were, a Russian, Persian, Indian, Turk, and Kalmuk Tartar.

June 18.—Mr. Hamilton wishing to proceed to England by Poland, Austria, and Germany, remained at Tabriz with Mr. Wilbraham, who purposed taking the same route. They set out together about a fortnight after me, and reached home a month later.

My future road being left to my own choice, I had recourse to the map, and selected that which seemed to offer the most novelty.

My mind made up, I immediately went to the Russian Chargé-d'affaires for advice and assistance. He tried to dissuade me from my scheme; but, seeing me determined, gave me a letter to a relation at Astrakhan, and countersigned the passport which had been given me by Major Willock. I discharged my old servant, a Turk, and substituted a native of Ghilaun, who could speak Persian and Turkish. I engaged five horses to carry my baggage and servants, and obtained from the Prince Royal a Mehmaundaur, with the usual *rukum*.

As the remainder of my route through Asia differs from that of nearly every preceding traveller, a short notice of it will be necessary.

I quitted the Persian, and entered the Russian territory, by crossing the river Arras, the Araxes of Plutarch. Between this river and the Kur (the ancient Cyrus or Cyrnus), is the beautiful province of Karabaugh, formerly the country of the Sacæ or Sacaseni, a warlike tribe of Scythians mentioned by Pliny and Strabo, and supposed to be the same people as our early ancestors the Saxons.

On quitting Karabaugh, I proceeded eastward through the province of Shirvan, the Albania of the Ancients,* the scene of many of the actions of Cyrus, and subsequently of Pompey the Great. The capital of this country is Nova Shumakhia, through which I passed on my road to Bakoo, a sea-port town in the same province on the western shore of the Caspian, the Casiphian sea of Scripture history. Hence I went north along the sea-shore through Daghestan, or "Region of Mountains," which name sufficiently denotes its character. Daghestan includes the states of Lezguistan, Shamkhaul, Durbund, and Tabasseran. The most important of these divisions is Lezguistan, a country inhabited by the most warlike tribe of Mount Caucasus, and which till within these few years was considered invincible. From Daghestan I passed through the pro-

* Vide Solin., Dionys. Hal., Justin, Strabo, Pliny, Pomp. Mela, Plutarch.

vince of Kumuk to Astrakhan, and entered Europe at the Russian town of Saritzin.

After this preamble I resume my daily narrative.

I left Tabriz in the evening of the anniversary of Waterloo, for Sheesha, the capital of Karabaugh. Major Monteith, Monsieur de Ambourger (Secretary to the Russian mission), and my old friend and fellow traveller Mr. Hamilton, accompanied me the first four miles; after which we commenced the ascent of a mountain, which led through so steep a defile as to oblige us frequently to dismount.

The appearance of the country for the first three days was a continuation of that description of scenery to which I had so long been accustomed—a succession of rugged eminences, intersected with valleys partially cultivated, but without a tree to relieve the dreary prospect.

After travelling sixteen miles, I felt an inclination to sleep, and, being now entirely my own master, I threw myself on my mattress, and in a moment was in a profound sleep by the road side.

June 19.—At seven we arrived at a small village on an eminence, called Shehruk, where we breakfasted, and halted for a few hours. In this neighbourhood the inhabitants were ploughing; though the soil was light and sandy, each plough was attended by two men and drawn by four oxen.

At 3 P. M. we set out, and in a distance of sixteen miles reached the village of Golijah, containing about forty huts. We soon collected a crowd about us; and the inhabitants, but especially the women, seemed to vie with each other in offering their assistance. The females wore no veils; they were handsome black-eyed damsels, low in stature, but of excellent proportion; their extreme plumpness was well set off by their large turbans, loose jackets, and capacious trowsers.

June 20.—After a sleepless night, welcome daylight at length arrived, to relieve me from the myriads of bugs, fleas, and other vermin. In a march of eight miles we reached Aher, a fortified town, commanded by Yusuf Khan, and garrisoned by three thousand Persians, who are organized on the European military system, by Russian deserters, fifty-seven of whom are at present in the town. One of them told me that the greater part of his countrymen had been here since the battle of Kertch, which took place in 1812, when the Persians gained a victory over the Russians on the banks of the Araxes.

At this place the Governor dismissed my old Mehmaundaur, and substituted one of his own followers. We left Aher at two in the afternoon, and halted for the night at a village called Hoja Kishlaukh, containing about ten wretched huts. I took up my quarters in a bullock-shed, in company with my horses; but this was a paradise compared to last night's lodging.

The road was, as usual, over a succession of mountains: a gentle breeze springing up at sunrise, rendered the morning cool and pleasant. We were now approaching the Russian frontier; and the Mehmaundaur particularly desired me to keep close to the baggage, on account of the banditti, who, he said, inhabited these mountains. We stopt to breakfast at Arabshehr, five miles distant from the last stage; a very pretty village, situate in a small but fruitful valley, and overhung with craggy mountains. My mat was spread in a cherry orchard; the boys climbed the trees for fruit, and the women brought bowls of milk, bread, and butter. We continued ascending till mid-day, when, arriving at the summit of the highest range of hills, a most beautiful scene suddenly and unexpectedly burst upon my view, rendered doubly interesting from having so long traversed a barren waste.

The sloping declivity of the mountain was beautifully covered with all kinds of forest trees; a rich underwood, the woodbine interwoven with the varied colours of other creepers, roses, aromatic shrubs and wild-flowers, rendered the scene sweet to the sense and grateful to the eye. From this point, might be seen successive ranges of mountains, decreasing in height until they marked the nearly level banks of the river Araxes. Abruptly rising on the extreme and broken line of the horizon, were the black and lofty mountains of the fruitful province of Karabaugh: large masses of rock in the foreground, appearing as if thrown up by some great convulsion of nature, completed the splendid variety of the scene.—We continued marching for several miles under the shade of a natural arbour, which, formed by the meeting of the trees, was sufficiently thick to protect us from the heat of the sun. The descent of this mountain was exceedingly steep, and not always devoid of danger; two of the horses fell twice.

In the course of the day we passed the beautiful little village of Yokhari Perasewaun, situate in the midst of corn-fields; and at sunset arrived at Gulakundee, a village in the mountain heights, where I bivouacked for the night on the roof of a house.

June 23.—I was again consigned to another Mehmaundaur. The road for seven miles led along the ridge of a mountain, overlooking a pleasant valley with abundant cultivation. The inhabitants were at this time busy in gathering in the wheat, which was in sheaves placed horizontally, and not vertically as in England. As the cattle proceeded slowly, I got off my horse to shoot, and in my walk was near treading on a snake. Upon describing it to the Mehmaundaur, he told me that it was probably a very venomous serpent called a *tulkha,* of which species there were numbers in the neighbourhood. The natives speak also of a spider, the bite of which is mortal, probably the *phalangium arenoides* of Linnæus. In the course of the day I saw three large snakes, and a small one resembling a cobra di capello.

The abundance of these venomous creatures illustrates the account given by Plutarch of Pompey the Great, who, after having overcome the Albanians between the Araxes and Cyrus, (consequently at a short distance hence,) wished to pursue the enemy to the banks of the Caspian Sea, but was compelled to abandon his design in consequence of the vast number of snakes and other reptiles which occupied the plains through which he would have been obliged to pass.*

* Gibbon doubts Pliny's account of the existence of venomous reptiles in this country.—Vide Decline and Fall of the Roman Empire, vol. iv. chap. xlvi. note 5.

As we descended towards the Araxes, the atmosphere became exceedingly sultry. The Mehmaundaur, to beguile the time, sang the " Loves of Furhaud and the Fair Shereen;" and that fertile theme of Persian songs, the Nightingale, the note of which he imitated with great correctness.

We reached the banks of the river at three in the afternoon, and proceeded to an encampment of the Laurijaumee tribe, whom we found occupied in manufacturing carpets and winding raw silk. We remained here till the cool of the evening, when we crossed the river Araxes (or, according to the present appellation, the Arras), which here separates the Persian from the Russian dominion.

The Araxes at this point is about one hundred yards wide: the rapidity of its course is much augmented by the confluence of mountain torrents, which, here rendering their tributary streams, throw up large isolated heaps of stone, and cause it to sweep along—"pontem indignatus Araxes." With motives probably similar to those which induced a noble poet to cross the Hellespont, I tried, but not with the same success, to swim over a river *once* celebrated as

> "The proud Araxes whom no bridge could bind."

In the mean while my servant and a party of Illyauts were transporting the baggage in a boat made of the hollow trunk of a tree, the fibres of which formed a rope to secure it to the bank. In this frail bark we crossed the river in perfect safety, at the same time that my horses, which had been made to swim over, had also arrived on the opposite shore, though one was nearly drowned by the rapidity of the current.

Some Illyauts, of the same tribe as those we had just left, occupied this bank of the river. I was here shown to the best tent, and a fine new carpet was spread for my accommodation.

The cattle had just been brought in for the night, and the promiscuous assemblage of man and beast was highly amusing. Before each tent the women were busily and variously employed, some in manufacturing carpets, others in milking cattle, and others in making bread of the same description as that mentioned in Scripture, as having been made by Sarah for the three Angels.

As I had now arrived in Russian territory, my Mehmaundaur delivered me formally over to the Chief of the encampment, from whom he took a written receipt for the safe consignment of my person.

The place occupied by this camp is a marshy swamp, extending several miles, called Meralian: myriads of musquitoes visited me as I retired to rest, but I slept soundly in spite of them, and at daylight set out for

Sheesha, the capital of Karabaugh. The inhabitants of this province, which in ancient maps is laid down as the country of the *Sacaseni*, the learned have tried to prove are from the same stock as the Anglo-Saxons.*

In a march of twelve miles we reached Peerhumud, a Tartar encampment, containing forty tents. We remained here two hours. Though the thermometer was 88 in the shade, and 122 in the sun, I felt but little inconvenience from the heat.

We put up vast numbers of partridges on our march, saw herds of antelopes, and swarms of locusts. We continued travelling till evening, when we fell in with a large body of Tartars, who had struck their tents for the summer season.

June 24.—We started at three in the morning. The appearance of the country has gradually improved, since we left the

* Turner's History of the Anglo Saxons, vol. i. p. 114.

marsh on the banks of the river. We travelled for several miles this morning completely protected from the heat of the sun by the luxuriant foliage of the trees. We passed a Cossack station to our left. A few straw huts comprised the barracks. The soldiers were employed in hay-making. As I passed, they all faced towards me, and stood at attention, with their heads uncovered, in compliment to my military dress. The country people also observed the European ceremony, by taking off their caps, which, discovering their shorn heads, had a curious appearance.

At some distance on the left hand we saw Khanakhi, a well-built town, in which is a Russian force. We passed several Armenian villages, all remarkable for their cleanly appearance. The cattle were now so knocked up that I almost despaired of reaching my destination. One of the horses, which was unable to proceed, was consigned to the care of an Armenian, and died shortly after.

On arriving at the summit of a mountain I came in sight of Sheesha. The town is built on a huge mass of sloping rock of great height. The ascent is so precipitous that the houses appear to be hanging on it like bird-cages. I was upwards of two hours in reaching the top. All the horses but two were completely knocked up. I took the least laden of these, and my servant and I rode by turns till we arrived at the gate. Unluckily I had left my passport with the baggage, which occasioned the sentinel to give me in charge of a corporal and a file of men, by whom I was conducted to the Russian officers' quarters, and afterwards to the house of the commanding officer of the regiment, where I remained for two hours in arrest.

My casual stay at the barracks gave me no great idea of the comfort of Russian subalterns. In a small dark dirty room I saw four beds: on each of which an officer was snoring as I entered.

It was now three o'clock in the afternoon: I had been for twelve hours employed in a laborious march, and for nineteen had not tasted food. I was almost worn out with heat, hunger and fatigue, and with but a faint hope of release, when something was said about assigning me a quarter. At this moment, a jolly fat-looking gentleman stepped forward, and begged for me as his guest. His name was Aga Beg; he was chief of the Armenians. With so fine a promise of good cheer as his appearance gave, I eagerly accepted his hospitality, and accompanied him home. A plentiful repast was spread on the floor. As soon as it was ready, two brothers of my host, the counterparts of himself, came in; and to judge by their appetites had, like myself, arrived half starved from a journey.

In the evening, two Missionaries came to call upon me; one a Swiss, the other a Pole. The latter was a Polish nobleman: his motive for leaving his own country was two-fold: the first was the laudable object of preaching the Gospel of Christ; the other was to attempt to establish liberty and equality wherever he went. He gave me a specimen of this visionary scheme, in inviting me to dinner the next day, and desiring to know whether I would object to sit at table with his servant, an Armenian of the lowest description. I told him I should be happy to dine with him, provided his servant should be behind a chair, and not in one.

June 25.—I dined with the Missionaries at one o'clock, and afterwards paid my respects to Colonel Tsichikoff, the Commandant of the district, who had just returned from visiting the different posts of the district under his command. Several officers were present during our interview, but, agreeably to Russian discipline, none sate in the presence of their superior officer. As neither the Colonel nor myself spoke any European language which the other understood, we were obliged to call in the aid of two Asiatic languages; he spoke Turkish, I Persian, and my servant acted as interpreter between us.

June 26.—The Commandant returned my visit the next morning, was very civil, and promised to do every thing in his power to facilitate my journey. He had not long taken his leave, when Aga Beg and his brother entered the room in high altercation, because the latter had allowed the Commandant to leave the house without partaking of a feast that had been prepared for him: this he considered a great affront; and so indignant was he at it, that he was very near going to the Colonel to persuade him to pay me another visit, solely for the purpose of making him eat some of the good cheer.

In the afternoon I accompanied one of the Missionaries over the town and the suburbs: in returning, he took me to the Armenian burying-ground. A boy who was with us ran forward, and kneeling down kissed one of the tomb-stones. Upon asking to whose tomb such honours were paid, I was told that it was that of a man named Nartuck, who is dignified with the title of Martyr, and respecting whom the following story is told and almost universally believed.

Forty years ago, when the Tartar *Khans* (Princes) were in possession of Sheesha, Nartuck, a Christian of Georgia, was the property of a Mahometan, whom he killed in attempting to commit a brutal assault upon his person. The brother of the deceased seized Nartuck, and gave him the usual alternative of suffering death or embracing Mahometanism. His belief in our Saviour and the Trinity was the only answer he made to the often-repeated proposal.

After undergoing the most dreadful tortures, he expired, and his body was conveyed to this spot. At night, a large flame appeared over the tomb, which was seen by both Mussulmans and Christians: one said it was fire from heaven, as a mark of divine wrath at an infidel having killed a Mussulman, and the others hailed it as a sign of the Deity's approbation of the conduct of the deceased: all parties, however, are agreed as to the fact. One with whom I conversed said he saw the flame, and described the size of it to me. Such an appearance might easily present itself without supernatural aid, in a country so abounding in bituminous productions.

Sheesha contains two thousand houses: three parts of the inhabitants are Tartars, and the remainder Armenians. The Tartars of the town, as well as of the whole province of Karabaugh, are of the Shiah sect of Mahometans. The present town was built eighty years ago by a Tartar prince: the remains of the old town are visible at the foot of the opposite hill. The lower parts of the houses are built of stone, with roofs, which are shelving, of shingle. The town and fort are surrounded by a wall; but the natural advantages of the situation, on the top of an almost inaccessible rock, have left little occasion for artificial defence. The language is a dialect of the Turkish; but the inhabitants, with the exception of the Armenians, generally read and write Persian. The trade is carried on principally by the Armenians, between the towns of Shekhi, Nakhshevan, Khoi, and Tabriz. The population was formerly greater than at present; but it is beginning to increase, as numbers of the inhabitants who fled from the oppressions of the Khans, are attracted back again by the milder yoke of Russia.

During my stay, the thermometer in the daytime ranged from 68° to 76°; the atmosphere in the town is 12 or 14 degrees cooler than the valley below.

The costume is much the same as the Persian; the greatest difference is in the head-dress. Instead of the small Persian cap, some of the Karabaughians have one as large as that worn by a French drum-major; others have a cap fitting close to the head, and bound round with fur.

June 27.—One of my host's brothers, whose inordinate addiction to eating and drinking had brought on a violent fit of indigestion, had applied to an Armenian doctor, who had recommended a double allowance of the strong bitter brandy he had been taking, and which was, no doubt, the original cause of his complaint. This prescription, as might be supposed, had only added fuel to the flame, and the poor fellow, gradually becoming worse, was at last in a burning fever.

In this dilemma, as Englishman and doctor are synonymous terms, he applied to me for assistance, which I gave by administering calomel, with the reckless profusion of an Indian operator. The dose was fortunately attended with most complete success; and so grateful was my patient for the relief I had occasioned, that instead of a fee he presented me with a Georgian silk handkerchief, a snuff-box, and a curiously wrought purse.

This cure soon spread my fame through the town, and brought numerous applicants for professional assistance. Defects of sight and hearing, and various other difficult cases, were laid before me, in the full confidence of obtaining instant relief. Amongst those willing to become my patients was a handsome young married woman, who began stating her ailments with such minuteness, that had I not interrupted her detail, I should soon have acquired more professional information from her, than I could have had the opportunity of communicating in return.

CHAPTER VIII.

Cossack Posts, Horses, Cheer—Mode of making Tea—Ruins of Berda—Abundance of Game—Lug—River Kur, the Ancient Cyrus—Koordameer—The Na-ib—Shumakhi—Interview with the Commandant—Town of Bakoo—Bazaar—Productions—Population—Military Force—Fire-Temple of Indian Pilgrims—A Brahmin—A Viragee—A Naphtha Well—My Servant knocked up—Cossack Officer—his Quarters—Breakfast—Town of Kuba—Kula noo—Fall asleep on Horseback—Flooded state of the river Samur—Lesguy Tartars—Russian Notion of English Radicalism—Major of Cossacks—City of Durbund—Ancient Walls—Population—Extensive Barracks—Russian Salutation—Dinner—My new Servant—His Appearance and Dress—His easy Manners—Polite Attention of my Host—Departure from Durbund—Nervous Irritability—Vexatious Delays—My Servant a Catcher of Tartars—His desisting from Sleep.

At the distance of every eight or ten miles, detachments of mounted Cossacks, with relays of horses, are stationed from Sheesha to Bakoo, and along the banks of the Caspian sea to Kizliar, a town skirting the great desert of Astrakhan. By the commandant of Sheesha I was furnished with an order on all these stations for five horses, to carry myself, servant, and baggage: I had besides, one, and occasionally two Cossacks, to escort me on the road, who also took back the horses at the end of the stage.

The Cossack horses here are stouter than those of the Don; they stand from twelve to thirteen hands, and are well calculated for the mountainous country in which they are principally used. The saddle is a frame-work of wood, much peaked before and behind; on this is strapped a black leather cushion, which serves the rider for his pillow at night: after a few days' riding I preferred this to the English saddle.

I started at six in the morning, and arrived at nine at the first Cossack station, the appearance of which did not impress me with any favourable opinion of Cossack comfort. Ten men were huddled together in a mud cabin, as closely as they could well be stowed; a few sheets of dirty paper formed a substitute for glass windows, which, if they admitted an imperfect light, so excluded the air, as to render the abode extremely hot and fulsome.

The men occupying the stations from Sheesha to Kizliar, are Cossacks of the river Terek. They are, I believe, on the same footing with those of the Don and Ukraine. They are free, serve for three years, receive no pay, but are fed: if their horses die, others are given them.

This day's march led us through as fine a country as any I had yet seen. Each turn of the winding road brought some new beauty to view; the trees which clothed the hills were entwined with wild vines, producing abundance of grapes. On quitting the mountains, we passed through extensive fields of corn, and we afterwards came on a spacious plain, over which vast herds of antelopes were bounding in every direction.

At sunset, having travelled about thirty miles, we forded the river Tartar, and halted for the night at a station so called. Being very hungry, I sent my servant to the Cossacks to purchase provisions; but he returned with the unwelcome intelligence, that black bread and the water of the river formed their only subsistence, and that even of such miserable cheer not a crumb remained. I fared well enough with Mahometans:—on arriving amongst Christians, I went supperless to bed.

June 29.—My object in coming to this station had been to visit some ancient ruins at a place called Berda; but I was informed that, Berda being out of the road, I could not be supplied with horses: I also heard that the regular stages to Bakoo were by Ganja, forty miles out of the direct line. These circumstances being duly weighed, and the cravings of an empty stomach thrown into the scale, determined me to forego for the present the advantages of my order for horses, and to take the shorter route through the Tartar villages, trusting to the inhabitants for safe conduct, and still hoping for more palatable fare than bread and water.

With some little difficulty, and a small *douceur*, the Cossacks agreed to send me as far as Berda, which I reached in a pleasant march of a couple of hours, along the banks of the river, through a beautiful forest of oaks, walnuts, and lime-trees. I found here a body of Tartars occupying some cane huts. Instead of indulging in idle curiosity, they all bustled about to prepare breakfast, and were so expeditious that I was well pleased with the resolution I had formed.

As every hint that will save time is useful to travellers, I strongly recommend my mode of making tea. I always carried my kettle at the bow of the saddle, and the moment I halted, the kettle was unloosed, and in it were put water, tea, milk and sugar, all together, making, when boiled, a very palatable beverage ; and I saved by this process, on an average, about an hour a-day.

While at breakfast the Mollah of the village paid me a visit, and conversed with me in Persian. Hearing that I came from India, he was particularly anxious to know any accounts relative to the Afghauns, who, he had heard, were the most warlike people of Hindoostan, with whom his tribe boasted a common origin. In my journey through the province of Shirvan, and the adjoining countries, questions respecting that nation were frequently asked me by the natives, and are worthy of remark, as they agree with the commonly-received opinion that a colony from ancient Albania (Shirvan) forms that tribe of Indian Tartars known by the name of the Afghauns. Amongst my notes I find the following extract from a book, but do not at this moment recollect the name of the author:—"The present Shirvan is the country of the ancient Albanians, conquered by Pompey; they are likewise called Alanians; and the Armenians, who never pronounce the letter l, who say Ghouka for Luka, and Ighia for Ilia, have called them Aghouani. These ancient Albanians have given up their country to the Turks, by whom it is now occupied, and have very probably formed the nation of the Afghauns, whom the Armenians acknowledge as their brethren, though their languages are now different, which may easily happen, and on which subject I think I have treated in my Primitive History."

The ruins at Berda are said to be very ancient; by some thought to be those of a city of Amazons, who, according to history, once inhabited this country; but while the existence of these female warriors is a matter of doubt, the site of one of their cities does not deserve much notice; nor indeed do the appearance of these ruins justify the assignment of an earlier date than the beginning of the Mahometan æra. A dilapidated wall running north and south, can be traced for upwards of a quarter of a mile. At the end of this, enclosed in a quadrangular fort, is a ruined mosque of glazed tiles, like that at Bagdad, attributed to Caliph Alraschid. Near the mosque I was shown some mounds, which were called the remains of Fire-temples; and a little further on was the tomb of a near relation of Mahomet, before which my guides fell on their faces, and remained prostrate for nearly a minute. The person here buried is said to have been the grand-niece of the Prophet, which, if true, would give to these ruins as remote a date as a thousand years.

We quitted Berda at eleven, and passed through a continuation of the forest. The game that I saw on this march is incredible: partridges were getting up every moment almost under the horses feet, and hares literally galloped in droves before us along the road.

I was informed that though the hare is forbidden to be eaten by the Mahometan law, both the Sunnis and Shiahs, inhabiting this country, have a dispensation from their priests, of which however they do not avail themselves, having a great dislike to the taste of that animal.

A traveller who is a sportsman, and not pressed for time, would find many modes of dissipating the tædium of his journey, as game of every description is most abundant, and as, I was told at Tabriz, the trout-fishing here is unequalled in any part of the world.

On leaving the forest we came to a small village called Lug, and thence went ten miles in an easterly direction, across a marshy plain, and arrived at dusk at Lumberan, where I became the guest of the Ket-khoda (the chief man) of the village.

June 30.—I started at sunrise, with fresh horses; and, having marched ten miles across a plain covered with antelopes, arrived on the banks of the Kur, which forms the southern boundary of the extensive province of Shirvan. This river, the Cyrus of the ancients, is considerably larger than the Araxes, but less rapid in its course: not far hence, it receives the waters of the Araxes, and the united streams then disembogue into the Caspian sea. It was on the banks of this river that Cyrus was massacred, together with his army, by the neighbouring mountaineers.

We hailed the village on the opposite side, and a boat was immediately sent, which conveyed us over. We here speedily procured horses, and proceeded to a village ten miles distant, of which I forget the name; where, after a delay of two or three hours, we engaged some horses at four times the usual charge. The weather throughout, was almost insupportable. The sun, which had been burning hot, took the breeze with it as it went down. As night came on, there was not a breath of air, and I had to pass through a swampy plain, nearly suffocated with heat, and devoured by musquitoes. I arrived at the village of Koordameer, a distance of thirty-four miles, and threw myself down to sleep in the first vacant space I could find.

July 1.—We travelled for fourteen miles over an uncultivated plain, covered with low brushwood, and came to a range of mountains, the base of which was for several miles studded with well-wooded villages, surrounded by extensive corn-fields. In the midst of these, stands a town, where a Cossack post is stationed. I called upon the chief person, who is called the Na-ib (deputy governor): he was seated in a garden, and dispensing justice as I arrived. He was a handsome Tartar, well informed, and of polite and easy address. Telling him I wished to proceed as quickly as possible, he immediately sent for my escort of Cossacks, and in a short time, set before me a comfortable meal of antelope venison.

The Na-ib pressed me very much to stay two or three days with him, that we might hunt together; but the wish to proceed onwards surmounted every other, and as soon as the horses arrived, I took leave of this hospitable Tartar.

The road hence led over mountains abounding in plentiful crops, but with nothing else in the appearance of the scenery to recommend it to notice: the range continued to Nova Shumakhi, where I arrived in the evening. This town, once the seat of government of a Tartar prince, though now in a dilapidated state, exhibits marks of former splendour; the buildings are principally of bricks, and the masonry is very good. It is defended by a quadrangular wall and a broad ditch. Like other towns in this turbulent region, it has felt the bad consequences of so often changing masters. Its present possessors, the Russians, are repairing the ravages inflicted by Aga Mohumud, who wrested it from the Tartars in the latter end of the last century. A new street of shops, on an European plan, is raising its head from amongst the remains of Asiatic architecture; and the places of Mahometan worship have been converted into storehouses and magazines. The place where I passed the night, had once been a Mudrissch, a Mahometan college, but now serves as a Cossack post-house.

July 2.—I had sent my passport to be sealed and countersigned by the Colonel-Commandant of this province, whose head-quarters are established here. In the morning it was brought me by one of his officers, with a civil message from the Commandant, desiring to see me, if not inconvenient. With the aid of one of his Meerzas (secretaries) who understood Persian and Turkish, the Commandant and I managed to converse, till, hearing I spoke French, he dismissed the Meerza, and sent for an officer who, he said, understood that language. An awkward silence of five minutes succeeded the entrance of this officer, who could neither interpret the Colonel's, nor understand my observations; at last, he stammered out "*le Colonel mange vous*," which I, supposing to mean an invitation to dinner, declined; and to relieve all parties, took my leave of the Colonel and this *professor* of the French language.

One of the stations at which I changed horses to-day, is situated in the midst of the ruins of the old Shumakhi, the Shumakha of ancient history: fragments of stone walls are still visible, and appear to extend a considerable distance, but I was not tempted to examine them more minutely.

July 3.—I slept at a Cossack station, and started at dawn of day for Bakoo. Our road was over a range of mountains, and as we reached the highest, the Caspian sea first came in sight, from which the sun was rising in splendid majesty.

We descended rapidly from hence into the low and arid plain, at the extremity of which is situated the sea-port town of Bakoo, where herds of double-humped camels were cropping the scanty pasture.

July 4.—Crossing over the drawbridge of the town, I was stopped by the officer of the main guard, to whom I delivered my passport; but, as reading was not one of his accomplishments, I had to wait in the sun till he could find some one to decypher the document. As at Sheesha, I was sent in charge of a file of men to the commandant's house, when, meeting the colonel of the engineers, who spoke French, I became his guest for the three days I remained here.

Bakoo, pleasantly situated on the peninsula of Abosharon, is a neat, though small seaport town, built entirely of stone. It is surrounded by a deep ditch and double wall of stone, the western side of which was completely carried away last year by one of those violent hurricanes so common in this place, and from which the name of the town is derived.* The roofs of the houses are flat, and covered with a thick coating of naphtha. There is one Armenian church, and twenty mosques; but some are in ruins, others have been converted by the Russians into magazines; and the only Russian church here was once a place of Mahometan worship.

The bazaar, which, though small and narrow, is neat and clean, forms an advantageous contrast with the general appearance of these Asiatic marts. There are no vege-

* Bakoo, Badko, "literally, the Wind of the Mountain; so named from the violent gusts of wind which blow at times from the chasms of the mountains."—Kinnier. —

tables here, nor, indeed, is there a blade of vegetation. The water, which is drawn from pits in the suburbs, is reckoned very wholesome. The principal productions are the black and white naphtha, which are in such abundance, that some of the wells are said to produce fifteen hundred pounds a-day. The principal commodities of commerce are common silk and small articles of Russian manufacture. The population is computed at four thousand souls, which, with the exception of a few Armenians, consists of Tartars. A force of five hundred men comprises the nominal strength of the garrison; but the mortality is so great, especially amongst the new conscripts, that they have seldom more than half that number effective.

In my evening strolls along the banks of the Caspian, I had occasion to observe the immense quantity of herrings which had been caught by the fishermen here. These fish, which are called by the Persians, the royal fish, were the finest of the species I had ever seen. I have little to remark respecting the Caspian sea, except that the answers to my enquiries confirmed what has been said of it by Pallas and other travellers.

On the site of the modern town, once stood a city, celebrated in the times of the Guebres for its sacred temples, on the altars of which blazed perpetual flames of fire, produced by ignited naphtha. To this place thousands of pilgrims paid their annual visit, till the second expedition of Heraclius against the Persians, when he wintered in these plains, and destroyed the temples of the Magi.* The fire which fed these altars continues to burn, and a temple is still inhabited by pilgrims, who, though not Guebres, still pay their adorations to the holy flames. To witness this, I had diverged

* Gibbon, vol. iv. chap. xlvi. page 520, fol. edit.

so great a distance from the usual route of travellers returning through Persia to Europe.

July 6.—I left Bakoo early this morning, attended by my servant and a Cossack. Sixteen miles north-east of the town, on the extremity of the peninsula of Abosharon, I came, after ascending a hill, in sight of the object of my curiosity. The country around is an arid rock. Enclosed within a pentagonal wall, and standing nearly in the centre of the court, is the fire temple, a small square building, with three steps leading up to it from each face. Three bells of different sizes are suspended from the roof. At each corner is a hollow column, higher than the surrounding buildings, from the top of which issues a bright flame; a large fire of ignited naphtha is burning in the middle of the court, and outside several places are in flames. The pentagon, which on the outside forms the wall, comprises in the interior nineteen small cells, each inhabited by a devotee. On approaching the temple, I immediately recognized, by the features of the pilgrims, that they were Hindoos, and not Persian fire-worshippers, as I had been taught to expect. Some of them were preparing food. I was much amused at the surprise they showed on hearing me converse in Hindostany. The language they spoke was so mixed up with the corrupt dialect of the Tartars, that I had some difficulty in understanding them. I dismounted from my horse, and gave it in charge to the Cossack, whom they would not allow to enter the temple, giving, somewhat inconsistently, as a reason, that he was an Infidel. I followed one of the pilgrims, who first took me into a cell where a Brahmin, for so his thread proclaimed him, was engaged in prayer. The constitutional apathy of the Indian was strongly marked in the reception this man gave me. The appearance of an armed European, it would be supposed, would have alarmed one of his timid caste; he testified, however, neither fear nor surprise, but continued his devotions, with his eyes fixed on the wall, not deigning to honour me with a look, till his prayers were over, when he calmly and civilly bade me welcome to his poor retreat.

My first acquaintance and the Brahmin then accompanied me round the other cells, which were whitewashed, and remarkably clean. In one of them was the officiating priest of the Viragee caste. This faquir wore only a small cloth round his loins; he held a piece of red silk in his right hand, and wore on his head a cap of tiger's skin: this is, I believe, emblematical of the life of the wearer, who, on leaving the society of man, is supposed to have recourse to the skins of wild beasts for a covering. In a small recess stood a figure of Vishnoo, and near it one of Hunoomaun,

——— "he
Whom India serves, the monkey deity."

My acquaintance with their deities seemed to please them much: one of them said, "You know our religion so well, that I need not tell you where you ought, or ought not to go." While I was here, another Viragee came in: he was a stout, well-looking man, with matted locks and shaggy beard, and covered with a coarse camel-hair cloth; his body was tattooed all over with the figure of Vishnoo.

On entering the temple he prostrated himself before the image. The priest then put into his hands a small quantity of oil, part of which he swallowed, and rubbed the rest on his hair. This man was once a Sepoy in the Indian army, and had been an orderly to a Colonel Howard in the time of Lord Cornwallis: he was the only man who seemed to have any acquaintance with the English. I was informed, that there is a constant succession of pilgrims, who come from different parts of India, and relieve each other every two or three years in watching the holy flame. This rule does not apply to the Pundit, or Chief, who remains for life. They spoke of their present chief as a man of great learning and piety: as they wished me very much to converse with him, I accompanied them to his cell, which was locked: they told me that he was either at prayers or asleep, but no one offered to disturb him. Of the pilgrims present, five were Brahmins, seven Viragees, five Sunapeys, and two Yogees. They spoke favourably of the Russians, but with more rancour against the Mahometans than is usual amongst Hindoos for those of a different persuasion. They said that Nadir Shah treated their predecessors with great cruelty; impaling them, and putting them to several kinds of tortures. All these faquirs were very civil and communicative, with the exception of one Viragee, the severest caste of Indian ascetics: he was quite a Diogenes in his way; and, when asked to accompany me, called out that it was no business of his.

Outside the temple is a well: I tasted the water, which was strongly impregnated with naphtha. A pilgrim covered this well over with two or three nummuds for five minutes; he then warned every one to go to a distance, and threw in a lighted straw; immediately a large flame issued forth, the noise and appearance of which resembled the explosion of a tumbril. The pilgrims wished me to stay till dark, to see the appearance at night; but the bright prospect of home in the distance got the better of curiosity, and made me hurry forward. I passed several villages, the inhabitants of which were employed in collecting black and white naphtha, and arrived at a Cossack station in the evening.

July 7.—In the first part of this march, the road led principally along the sea-shore; the country, throughout, is a salt desert, which continues till within twenty versts of Kuba.

In my anxiety to proceed at a quicker pace, I so completely knocked up my servant, that he could with difficulty be prevented from falling out of his saddle. After a hot and fatiguing march, we arrived at a Cossack station, where I purposed breakfasting; but my exhausted domestic had no sooner dismounted, than he threw himself into the first shady spot he could find, and was soon in a profound slumber, leaving me without breakfast, or the power to make known my wants. Thinking I should only lose time by disturbing the poor fellow's rest, I let him sleep on, and sate down on my baggage, hungry and dispirited. In this mood I was accosted by a gigantic personage, whose face, studded with pimples, was curiously set off by his huge Tartar cap. The rest of his person was incased in a cloak formed of undressed sheepskins, with the wool worn inside. He turned out to be the officer of the station, and was one of those Cossacks who visited Paris in 1815; and whose Tartar skill in spoliation must be still fresh in the recollection of the Parisians.

In a friendly growl, which he intended to be French, I distinguished the word *déjeûner:* immediately at the sound, I followed him into a wretched hovel, to which he welcomed me with an apologetic sigh. The chamber was about twelve feet square, and lighted by three small panes of glass and a few sheets of oiled paper; an uniform coat, a pair of pantaloons, a sabre, a cartouch-box, and a pair of pistols, suspended from several nails, were the only decorations of the mud walls; and a bed of straw, with the black saddle cushion for a pillow, formed the couch of the warrior. For the humble appearance of the dwelling I had been prepared; but bitter was the disappointment on observing the meal which he had dignified with the name of *déjeûner*. Bread, the blackest and heaviest I ever tasted; water not of the cleanest, three cucumbers, and a tough strip of salt fish, formed this morning's sorry bill of fare.

After breakfast, I returned to my servant, and sate watching his eyes for two hours, which, in my impatience, I thought never would re-open. At length he awoke, and with the assistance of a hearty shake, which I gave to prevent a relapse into drowsiness, he was so far recovered as to be hoisted into the saddle, and we again got under weigh.

From this day to that on which we parted, the poor Persian became worse than useless; as, instead of his being of any assistance to me, I had to wait upon him, and to use every means of persuasion to induce him to continue the journey. On arriving at the end of the stage, I discovered that I had left behind me the order for horses, but the serjeant on the station, after making a few difficulties, which were silenced by a small fee, allowed me to proceed. I halted at a Cossack station, after a cool moonlight ride along the seashore.

July 7.—The appearance of the country improves as we approach the district of Kuba, the most fertile part of Shirvan. The villages are thickly inhabited, and the cultivation abundant.

July 8.—At mid-day I reached Kuba, once the residence of a Tartar Khan, but now in possession of the Russians, who have here a garrison of three thousand men.

Kuba stands in an elevated situation on the banks of the river Deli, a rapid stream, which, issuing from the Caucasus, flows into the Caspian Sea. Except towards the river, the steep banks of which are a sufficient protection, the town is defended by fortified walls. The population is computed at about five thousand souls, one-third of which are Jews. As I had no order for horses, I applied to the commandant for assistance, who, saying that the Cossack horses were most probably engaged on public employ, gave me an order, in Turkish, on the villages.

The country, for several versts, is populous, well cultivated, and abounding in wood and water. I passed through a forest of lofty trees, and saw large parties of soldiers employed in felling timber for building. After fording a river, I came to a commanding eminence, called Kula Noo, (New Fort,) where two hundred Russian soldiers were employed in building barracks on a very extensive scale.

From the first setting out in this expedition, I had tried in vain to shake off the painful feeling of drowsiness with which I had always been assailed at some period of the day's march. This evening, however, I fell sound asleep in my saddle for three hours; and though the road led over precipitous mountains, I did not awake until

I had arrived at the station, when I was roused by the Cossacks, who had spread my mattress for me in the middle of the yard.

July 9.—I found here three Cossack officers, who informed me that, had I been able to have forded the river Samur at the usual place, I should have reached Durbund in a journey of forty versts, but the river had become so swelled by the sudden melting of the snows on Mount Caucasus, that I should be obliged to travel double the distance.

I proceeded a considerable way along the banks of this angry torrent, and afterwards passed through several villages. At one of them I met with an officer in charge of specie for the troops; finding we were both about to cross the river, I breakfasted with him, and then accompanied him to the water's edge. The country, as we proceeded, was extremely flooded, and our progress slow in consequence of the difficulty of getting the treasure-waggons through the muddy ground.

We forded the river at about twenty-five versts from the last station, but the torrent was running with such violence, that we were nearly three hours in reaching the opposite bank, which we could not have done without the timely assistance of the neighbouring mountaineers. The Samur, ancient *Albanus*, is three hundred and fifty yards wide, and not more than four feet deep; large heaps of stone are dispersed over the surface, and render the passage rugged and dangerous. In crossing the Samur we quit the province of Shirvan, and enter on the southern boundary of Lezguistan. In the natives of this country, we again fall in with a tribe possessing the same wandering and predatory habits as the numerous hordes which I have passed in the course of this journey. The Lesguis are reckoned the bravest people of Mount Caucasus. Till within a very few years, they proved most formidable enemies to their Russian neighbours; but now, owing to the late encroachments of the latter nation, they are in a state of subjection. They occasionally, however, make a gallant stand in defence of the liberty they had enjoyed from time immemorial. When I was at Tabriz, I had heard of a Russian force being sent against the Lezguis, and I had expected, on my arrival here, to find that the two countries were engaged in war; but I was one day set right by a Russian officer, who, alluding to the expedition against the Lezguis, said, that the affair was a mere trifle; which, by way of illustration, he compared to our mode of quelling an English insurrection, when we occasionally send "a brigade of troops against Hunt and his army of Radicals."

Once, on the opposite shore, I quitted the convoy of my comrade, and proceeded at a quicker rate over a well-cultivated country. Reapers, consisting entirely of females, were gathering in the harvest. In one spacious field I saw no less than a hundred women at work. In the evening I bivouacked, as usual, at a Cossack station.

July 10.—In the morning the sergeant was very impertinent; would pay no attention to my Tartar order for horses, and would not furnish me with any. Soon after, a Major of Cossacks, a personage with a round hat and a long beard, and attended by an orderly, rode up, and, on hearing the sergeant's story, supported him in his refusal. As the major was very haughty and uncivil, I put on as big a look as I could assume, and, producing my passport with the signatures of several Russian commandants, told him to decline furnishing me with horses at his peril. This blustering had the desired effect, for the major muttered a few words, looked exceedingly foolish, and then galloped away, leaving me for a moment in doubt of my application ; but this was soon dispelled by the sudden appearance of the sergeant with the horses, who, with a crest-fallen look, and in the most submissive manner, held the stirrup for me to mount. This major is nearly the only Russian officer from whom I experienced uncivil treatment.—I changed horses ten versts distant, and at mid-day reached Durbund. I immediately reported myself to the Commandant, who, in the most hospitable manner, assigned me a good quarter, introduced me to his lady, and invited me to dine and breakfast with him during my stay. In the afternoon he sent me one of his horses, and accompanied me in a ride over the town.

The modern capital of the province of Durbund, Daghestan, stands on the site of the city of Albania, and corresponds in position with the *Albaniæ pylæ* of the ancients. The walls, which are of undoubted antiquity, are visible from the height of the mountain, and, by the appearance of the water, may be traced a considerable distance into the Caspian Sea. These divide the city into three compartments; the highest, comprising a square of half-a-mile, constitutes the citadel. The town is in the centre, and there are a few gardens in the lower division. Near the sea, I was shown the foundation of a house built by Peter the Great, who visited this city soon after it had been taken by the Russians. The highest portion of the walls is in the middle division, and is about thirty feet high, twenty thick at the foundation, decreasing to twelve in the upper part, over which is a parapet three feet thick.

The walls are built of a compact stone of a dark colour, and consist of large blocks: the cement which binds them together, is concealed by the insertion of a narrow slip of stone between each. Sixty bastions protrude at regular intervals. One of the gates towards the north, probably that which had been most in ruins, has lately been repaired by the Russians, who have adorned it with an inscription in their language: the new work sets off to advantage the more ancient appearance of the other parts of the buildings. Over another of the gates, is an inscription by Chosroes, King of Persia, in whose possession it was prior to the Mahometan æra; and so impressed was he with the importance of the place, that he granted the governors the privilege of sitting on a golden throne, which once gave a name to the city. There are various conjectures as to the founder of these walls, though all are agreed upon their high antiquity. Some say they are the celebrated Gog and Magog of history; others, that they were founded by Alexander the Great, though it seems quite improbable that he could ever have come so far as this place. There are others, again, who affirm that the founder was another Alexander, who flourished several centuries before the

Macedonian hero. The universal belief among the Orientals is, that the wall formerly extended hence to the Black Sea; and though the Russian officers told me that remains have been seen in the Caucasus to a great distance, I have the authority of Major Monteith (who has frequently attempted to discover them), that no traces whatever are visible in any part of Georgia. The most probable conjecture appears to be, that the wall terminates in some strong feature of the Caucasus, and was built for the purpose of closing this pass against the invasion of the northern Tartars.

In more modern times, Durbund has alternately been in the hands of Turks, Tartars, Arabs, Persians, and Russians; the latter nation having now possession of it for the second time. The number of the inhabitants, independent of the Russian garrison, is estimated at twelve thousand; and comprises a mixed population of Armenians, Georgians, Mahometans, principally of the Sunni persuasion, and of Jews; of which religion there are great numbers along the coast, and, as I am informed, throughout the interior of Mount Caucasus.

The bazaar is tolerably good, but the houses are mean and poor. I understand that General Yermōloff, the commander-in-chief of Georgia, intends pulling down the old town and building it anew. To the south of the town is a large tract of cultivated land, laid out in corn fields and vineyards; and there are some gardens which produce abundance of a variety of fruits, the white mulberry among others; a great quantity of saffron is also grown here. My guides took me to the burying-ground, as many of the tombs are said to be very ancient. The tomb-stones are round blocks of marble, with inscriptions in the Cufic character. Several were pointed out as belonging to some Tartar princes, who died in this spot with sword in hand, while fighting in defence of their religion.

July 11.—This morning (Sunday) the Commandant took me to dine with the colonel of a regiment quartered in the neighbourhood. The colonel received me with much politeness, and introduced me to his lady, a lively and pretty Livonian, who, I was pleased to find, spoke French fluently. The officers as well as the men occupied temporary buildings, made of the branches of trees; but barracks on an extensive scale were preparing for their reception. While dinner was getting ready we went round the buildings, which are all of stone, and will have a grand appearance. This work is performed entirely by the soldiers; and the colonel informed me, that there was not a man in the regiment who did not follow some trade. On my return to the room, the company, consisting of the officers of the regiment and the staff-officers of the garrison, were thronging in. I here saw, for the first time, the Russian salutation. Every officer, on entering, took the right hand of the hostess and pressed it to his lips, while she at the same moment kissed his cheek. Dinner was prefaced by a glass of brandy and a piece of salt-fish. The ladies, of whom there were several, seated themselves together: the post of honour next our fair hostess, was assigned to me as the stranger; the band played during dinner; after which the company (with the exception of myself, who took a siesta,) sat down to cards.

July 12.—My Persian servant, hearing I intended to resume the journey this afternoon, told me that he would not, for any sum that I could offer, accompany me again; but as I had also determined that nothing should induce me to take him further, I had, with the assistance of the Commandant, provided myself with a substitute, who made his appearance this morning ready equipped for the march. He was a tall, fearless-looking Tartar, upwards of six feet high, with large, fierce black eyes, an aquiline nose, and a pair of mustaches that nearly covered his face. His dress, the same as that worn by other Lezguy Tartars, consisted of a low cap fitting close to the head and bound round with fur, which being of the same colour as his mustaches, heightened the ferocity of his weather-beaten features. A robe of blue stuff extended to the knee; on each breast were fixed a row of painted cartridge cases; a narrow leather strap bound his loins, and in it were stuck a flint, a steel, a small tobacco-pipe, a handsome dagger, a pair of pistols, and a Tartar whip, consisting of two thick thongs. On his feet he wore a sort of sandal, which was fixed on with lacings bound tightly round the leg up to the knee. This, I have observed, is common to the mountaineers of Coordistan and Persia, as well as throughout the line of Caucasus, and is probably of use in supporting the muscles of the leg when ascending a height. The crossed pattern of the Scotch Highlander's tartan hose, may possibly have some allusion to this mode of binding.

In mentioning my Tartar's equipment, I had almost forgotten the most material article, for such he considered it—a quart bottle of Russian arrack, to which he always resorted on the journey, as his only and infallible cure for hunger, thirst, and fatigue.

The free and easy manner of this fellow towards myself was curiously contrasted with the respectful deportment to which I had been accustomed from his predecessor, who never addressed me but with the title of Jenaub (excellency), nor spoke of himself but as my bundah (slave).

My stipulation with the Tartar was that he should accompany me to Kizliar, and for this he should receive a tomaun a day, provided he was always on the alert, and was content with the small portion of sleep I should allow him. He immediately replied, that he would not sleep at all; a promise which, to the best of my belief, he faithfully kept. The bargain was scarcely concluded, when the Persian, in an earnest tone of remonstrance, spoke a few words to him in Turkish, which I found were intended to dissuade him from accompanying me, saying that, if he did, he would certainly die of fatigue. In reply to this friendly caution, the Tartar cast a contemptuous glance at his adviser, and turning round familiarly to me loudly exclaimed, "God be praised, *we* are not Persians!"

As a small acknowledgment for the truly kind and hospitable behaviour of the Commandant towards myself, I made him a present of my pistols; and he in return gave me a handsome Lezguy dagger, and a curious segar tube. At two o'clock we sate down to a farewell dinner; after which, as I was preparing to take my leave, several ladies of the garrison, attracted perhaps by curiosity, came to see the English officer: at this I was of course well pleased, as it gave me an opportunity, at parting, of practising the Russian mode of salute.

I had ordered the baggage to be packed, and every thing to be got ready by four o'clock. At the appointed hour, my Tartar arrived with six men, whom the Commandant had sent to escort me to the first Cossack station, commanded by a Major, his particular friend, to whom he gave me a letter of introduction. This stage was only ten miles; but, my object in leaving Durbund in the afternoon being to avoid the probable detention at the barrier in the morning, I accepted the Major's invitation to sup with him, and take up my quarters for the night.

July 14, 15.—I find a chasm of these two

days in the notes of the journal; an omission attributable to the anxiety I felt to hurry forward on the journey, which sensation superseded every other, and rendered me as incapable of mental exertion, as insensible to bodily fatigue. In this nervous state I could find but little time for meals and rest, and still less for paying the necessary attention to the objects of interest on the march. Thus I continued travelling night and day, availing myself of the occasional delay in changing horses to procure a few hours' sleep.

Notwithstanding the hurry I was in, our progress was but slow. Vexatious delays were sure to occur at every stage, the Cossack posts not having been long established: at one place, the horses were out in the fields; at another, they had just arrived from a stage; in short, I had frequently to lament, that though always a great loser of patience, I was not often a proportionate gainer of time.

With no such stimulus to exertion as that by which I was actuated, my indefatigable servant was fully as much on the alert as myself during the march, and, as I said before, never slept a wink during our occasional halts. This habit of wakefulness he had acquired as a "Catcher of Tartars;" a situation in which he had been employed by General Yermoloff, when the road was infested by the Lezguy hordes.

Though I have no notes, I remember arriving on the night of the 14th at a Cossack station, where, as was my custom, I reclined with my face towards the east, that I might have the advantage of the sun's earliest rays to rouse me from slumbers which a restless spirit grudgingly considered as so much lost time.

As I was about to fall asleep, the bright

light of the moon was reflected on the huge figure of the Tartar. He was sitting by my pillow, a bottle of arrack was in his lap, and his glaring eyes were watching mine. At dawn of day I awoke, and beheld him seated exactly in the same position; and, but for the evident diminution in the contents of the bottle, I should have given him credit for having stirred neither hand nor foot.

CHAPTER IX.

District of Shamkhaul—The Shamkhaul—Tarkee—A little Amazon—River Koi Soui—Extraordinary Flight of Locusts—Nogai Tartars—Quarantine-house—Arrive at Kizliar; am the guest of a friend of my Servant's—The Town, Population, and Produce—My new Servant, a Jew boy—Anecdote—Departure from Kizliar—My new Equipage—Post-horses, Cossack and Kalmuck Drivers—Locusts in the Desert—Quarantine—Arrival at Astrakhan—Scotch Missionary-house—Alexander Cassim Beg—Obstacles to the Missionaries—Their Privileges—City of Astrakhan—Population—Variety of Costume—Prisoner begging—Russian Charity—Trade—Salt—Productions—Indecent Custom—Sturgeon Fishery.

July 16.—We passed through the populous and beautiful district of Shamkhaul, the name of which formerly gave the title to the Prince of the country. The present representative of the family, though stripped of his authority by the Russians, is indulged by them with the honorary rank of Lieutenant-general in their army, and with the permission to retain the appellation of his ancestors.

The capital of this district is Tarkee; but the Shamkhaul himself resides in a romantic village, situate on the brow of an eminence, which commands a beautiful view of undulating mountains clothed with trees, and verdant valleys traversed by numerous rills.

My Tartar had so excited my curiosity by a description of the Shamkhaul, that I diverged from the direct road to see him, and, on my arrival, presented him with a letter from the friendly Commandant of Durbund, which I hoped would procure me an invitation to dinner, as my servant had particularly enumerated a love of good living among his estimable qualities.

In this scion of a royal stock, who is celebrated for eating a whole sheep at a meal, I beheld an unwieldy, red-bearded Tartar, with a forbidding countenance, that at once destroyed all hopes of a dinner. Our interview was short; he was nearly the first uncivil Mahometan I had met, so I lost no time in remounting my horse, and tried at parting to return with interest the cavalier deportment with which I had been received. I did not arrive at Tarkee till four o'clock the following morning, having been twenty-two hours on the march.

July 17.—I resumed the journey after five hours' rest, and did not stop to look at Tarkee, which contains a garrison of Russians: it is considered half way between Kizliar and Durbund. I crossed the Tarkali-oozan, and arrived at a small village in the afternoon.

On dismounting, my stirrup was held by a fair and handsome-looking person, who proved to be a female. Admiration of a military life had induced her to deprive herself of her fair tresses, and to wear the dress of a man, preparatory, as she said, to offering her services to the Emperor as a soldier. Hearing I was in the army, she told me, that, if she had been a little older, she would have accompanied me. I told her that she would be rejected, from her feminine appearance; but she said, she would cut off her breasts, whenever they were too large for concealment. On taking leave of this little Amazon, I gave her an old aiguillette, which she accepted with great delight, and strutted off with it on her shoulder, to the no small amusement of the villager.

At midnight I reached the River Koi Soui, which divides a large Tartar village, occupied by a party of Russians. The commanding officer of the detachment (a lieutenant) had been in bed some time, but, hearing of my arrival, ordered refreshments to be prepared; and such was his strict sense of discipline, that nothing would induce him to be seated in the presence of one he considered his superior officer.

July 18.—We crossed the river in the morning, and marched thirty versts in a northern direction over a level plain.

Looking towards the east, I observed an opaque body moving gradually forward. It was a flight of locusts, so large as to have the appearance of a black cloud extending over the horizon. "They covered the face of the whole earth, so that the land was darkened." These winged strangers, more formidable than the banditti of the country, had destroyed every blade of vegetation, and had turned a well-cultivated plain into a desolate waste.

The Nogai Tartars, with whom we now were, differed in features from the handsome tribes occupying the countries we had just quitted. They had thicker lips, flatter noses, smaller eyes, and that peculiar expression of countenance common to their race. Scattered over the plain were several large encampments of bell-shaped tents, which had a very picturesque appearance.

In the afternoon, I arrived at the Quarantine-house, a small fort surrounded by an inconsiderable ditch. I wished to have continued my journey, but the commandant, though he said he would not detain me, was so pressing in his invitation, that I halted for the night.

July 19.—I reached Kizliar, only ten versts distant, at an early hour. Not knowing where to find a lodging, I followed my servant, who offered me the hospitality of a friend. As I had not much faith in his promise of good cheer, I was agreeably surprised on seeing him stop at a neat and spacious house, where a respectable Armenian received and ushered me into a clean and comfortable apartment.

This being a fast-day, no meat was allowed to be sold at the shops; but these rules of abstinence not always applying to the commandant, who, doubtless, thinks his office entitled to a dispensation, my host very kindly procured from him some mutton, which seasoned by some excellent red champagne, of Kizliar growth, afforded an entertainment to which I had long been unaccustomed. The town of Kizliar, standing on the banks of the river Terek, is sixty versts from the Caspian Sea. The population, including those of the dependent villages, may be computed at twenty thousand. Of these the Tartars and Armenians form the two greatest divisions; the rest of the inhabitants are the refuse of the numerous tribes of Mount Caucasus. The grapes of Kizliar produce several different kinds of wine; indeed the vines grown on the banks of the Terek, are equal in quality to those of the Don. The inhabitants cultivate also cotton and tobacco, but import the greater portion of their corn from Astrakhan.

July 20.—As Kizliar is the last Cossack station on the road, here ended my journey on horseback: horses and carriages are procured hence to St. Petersburg. Being resolved to proceed with as little possible delay, I asked the commandant for an order for post-horses, but he refused to let me go without being attended by some one whom he could hold responsible for my safety. As it would have been cruel to have again accepted the services of my Tartar, who, poor fellow, had scarcely awoke from the sleep he commenced the morning before, I offered a reward to any one who would become my travelling companion to Astrakhan, and soon succeeded in engaging a Jew boy in that capacity.

The rude customs of my Tartar friends are exemplified in an anecdote respecting this new servant, which, I confess, it gives me pleasure to relate, though I make a considerable figure in it.

He is a native of a small remote village on the banks of the Terek, whence his sister, a beautiful girl twelve years old, was carried off by some Tartar kidnappers, who sold her to a Mahometan merchant resident here. The poor Jew, after an unsuccessful application to the commandant for her release, flew to the merchant, who agreed not to make her his wife for two years, and in the interval to return her for a specified sum. The time had nearly elapsed when I saw him. The money I gave was sufficient for his sister's release; and I feel somewhat proud of having relieved this fair damsel.

At four o'clock in the afternoon, my new equipage came to the door, driven by a Kalmuck Tartar. The vehicle was an open four-wheeled carriage, without springs, called an *Arba.* It was five feet five inches long, three feet broad, and perhaps three deep, resembling a beef-barrel sawed in half. To this wretched conveyance were attached three half-starved ponies abreast. The collars were of wood, and the reins and traces of rope. Over the collar of the centre horse were suspended three bells. Not a moment was lost in packing the baggage. A little straw was placed at the bottom, the mattress was spread on it, and the clothes-bags served as pillows. We were no sooner seated than off we went, full gallop, to the jingling of the bells; our party consisting of the master, a Christian, the valet, a Jew, and the coachman, a worshipper of the Grand Lama.

Quitting the suburbs of Kizliar, you immediately enter on the great desert of Astrakhan. The road hence to the city is tolerably good, with the exception of some high sandy ridges, which require you to take a circuitous route.

We reached the first post-house at dark: I here found the utility of the bells, which had so annoyed me before. Their sound being heard at a considerable distance in the stillness of the desert, warns the keeper of the post-house of the traveller's approach, and enables him to bring in the relay horses from pasture. The man employed in this office was mounted on a horse without saddle or bridle: he had a long two-pronged stick in his hand, and drove before him about thirty horses, which obeyed him as readily as a pack of hounds do the voice of a huntsman.

With the exception of the keepers of the post-house, no population was visible till within the vicinity of Astrakhan. In the winter, twenty-four thousand families encamp here, and retire in the summer season to the different branches of Mount Caucasus.

The post-houses, which are most miserable dwellings, are kept either by Cossacks or Kalmucks. The contrast between the representatives of these two nations was highly amusing. At one stage I was driven by a shaggy, unshaved Russian, in a European hat. At the next, my coachman was a lank-haired, beardless Kalmuck, in yellow cap and scarlet boots. Each driver was very sparing of his whip. If the horses flagged, he commenced a song, which, like the melody of Orpheus, so charmed the brutes, that they always quickened their pace. There was but little harmony in the performances of either Cossack or Kalmuck ; but I forgot the toil of the journey in listening to the whine and hum of the one, and the gay and sprightly air of the other.

July 22.--The only change from the sand of the desert, which for two days we had now been traversing, was here and there a patch of rank grass. On these forlorn vestiges of verdure the hungry locusts had settled in swarms; not to be disturbed by our carriage-wheels, which rolled over them with as little scruple as the car of Juggernaut crushes a devotee.

At midnight I arrived at the Quarantine-house, where I heard I should be detained four days. I found here three Kizliar merchants, who had passed me in a kibitka.

July 23.—I wrote a letter to the Governor of Astrakhan in the morning, which brought me a release in the afternoon; but my three companions had to remain in confinement during the whole period.

We reached Astrakhan, a distance of twelve versts, in an hour's drive. We crossed a branch of the river Wolga, on which the city is built. After a slight detention at the custom-house, we were allowed to proceed in any direction we chose. My Jew servant, who had not long left his village on the banks of the Terek, and had always considered Kizliar as the greatest of cities, was so confounded at the populous appearance of Astrakhan, that he could not say a word, and left me to find my way about as I could. The Kizliar merchants had spoken of *Khanee Fering*, an English inn: by repeating these words, I was at last directed to a spacious house, at the door of which was playing a rosy-cheeked boy, whose features were so English that I spoke to him in our own language. He told me he was the son of the Rev. Mr. Glen, and that this was the Scotch Missionary-house. I had scarcely recovered from the satisfaction of hearing the welcome accents of my native land, when his mother, a handsome woman, begged I would come up-stairs, and remain with her family during my stay. I partook of a slight refreshment, and soon after there was a general summons to prayers. The congregation consisted of twenty English persons, including women and children. Psalms were first chanted. One of the missionaries then put forth an eloquent extempore prayer to the Almighty, into which he introduced a thanksgiving for my safe arrival and escape from so many dangers.

At no period of my life do I remember to have been impressed with so strong a feeling of devotion as on this evening. Few persons of the same general habits will understand my particular feelings. Few have ever been placed in the same situation under similar circumstances. Quitting countries once the most rich and populous, now the most desolate and lone, fulfilling in their calamities the decrees of Divine Providence; safe from the dangers of the desert, and from the barbarian tribes with whom every crime was common, I found myself in a religious sanctuary among my own countrymen, in whose countenances, whatever were the trivial errors of their belief, might be traced the purity of their lives, and that enthusiasm in the cause of religion which has caused them to become voluntary exiles: whose kindness promised me every comfort, and whose voices were gratefully raised to Heaven in my behalf.

July 24.—After breakfast I was introduced to Alexander Cassim Beg, a Persian of rank, who had been converted by these missionaries from the Mahometan to the Christian faith. He is a fine, intelligent young man, and speaks English with great fluency: he is nearly the only Mussulman who has had the courage to acknowledge his conversion. Several others, equally convinced of their errors, do not forsake them, from a fear of the consequences. The missionaries are met by almost insurmountable obstacles. The person changing his religion, ceases from all intercourse with his countrymen: he must choose his companions from the natives of a foreign land, with whose habits and language he is unacquainted: if a mechanic, no one gives him employment; if a merchant, the only excuse for dealing with the apostate is an intent to defraud him.

The Scotch missionaries at Astrakhan belong to a colony in Circassia, or, more properly speaking, Cabardia, named Karass. The affairs of the colony are managed by their own laws, except in criminal cases. They have a free exercise of their own religion, and have liberty to receive into their communion converts from amongst either Mahometans or heathens. They are exempt from military service, and from having soldiers quartered on them. They pay no taxes, except about five copecks for each acre of arable land; this is not paid by the individual, but by the community. They may travel all over Russia with their own passports, and may leave the empire when they choose. They have power to purchase slaves (not being

Russians or Georgians), with the understanding that they are free at the end of seven years. At the first establishment of the colony, a number of Mahometans were purchased, or, as they call it, ransomed. A Circassian, christened John Mortlock, and one or two others whom I saw at Astrakhan, are of this description; but the Society not approving of this plan, the privilege has not been acted upon for many years.

Astrakhan stands at the mouth of the river Wolga, on an island formed by two of its branches. The island is called Zauchy Baugor (a Hare's Seat.) The city is inclosed within a fortified wall, but the water may be said to define its natural boundary. A navigable canal traverses it in various parts. A person so recently arrived from the mud palaces of Persia, is not perhaps well qualified to speak of the state of this place. To me it appeared clean and well built; its streets broad and commodious, its houses lofty and regular: I saw it, however, under considerable advantage. In consequence of the expected arrival of the Emperor Alexander, the inhabitants had whitewashed their houses, roofs and all, by order of the government. The cathedral, a magnificent building, with its green cupolas, is the most beautiful object here, and may be seen at the distance of sixty versts by traders approaching from the Caspian sea. In the middle of the town is the principal square, about two hundred yards wide N. and S., and one hundred E. and W. On the east are the houses of the Governor and Vice-Governor. Opposite is the house occupied by the missionaries. On the south is a Gostenoi Dvor, or range of shops, which, being uniform, have a pleasing and grand appearance. A new Gostenoi Dvor is now erecting a little to the west of the square. The natives of every country enjoy religious toleration here. The town is full of temples of Hindoos and Kalmucks, of the mosques of Mahometans, and of the churches of different Christian sects. Astrakhan is considered as the see of the Armenian Archbishop in Russia: I believe there is no other north of the Caucasus.

The city contains a population of sixty thousand Russians, numerous tribes of Tartars, Armenians, Indians, Kalmucks, and natives of Bokhara. As every one retains the dress of his country, the grand square at the time of daily market has a very picturesque appearance. It was curious to observe so great a variety of costume and feature crowded into so small a space. I was delighted again to hear the fair sex enjoying one of their greatest privileges, that of speech, which they here used with noisy volubility, in haggling their wares with the natives of nearly every Asiatic country. While watching the various groups, I saw a prisoner, heavily ironed and guarded by a file of men, going round the market begging; numbers gave him a trifle. It was amusing to observe the ceremonious behaviour of the giver and receiver on these occasions. Both took off their hats, made a profusion of low bows, and then embraced each other with a politeness that accorded oddly with their half-savage appearance.

Charity is a very prevalent virtue amongst the Russians, though they appear to care little whether the object be worthy or not. I have not unfrequently seen a Russian give a coin of five farthings value to a professed beggar, who returned him two farthings in exchange.

The eastern shore of the Wolga, along the city and suburbs, is lined with vessels for two versts. Of these, some belong to the Caspian trade, but the greater portion to the inland navigation. Foreign trade is carried on chiefly by Russians and Armenians, but for the most part in Russian and Astrakhan vessels. Few towns can boast of a more advantageous situation for the purposes of commerce. The Wolga, which is three versts broad opposite Astrakhan, is navigable hence to St. Petersburg, the passage varying from fifty-six to about seventy days. Several of the missionary families came from Leith to Astrakhan by water.

In the government of Astrakhan, the salt-trade is carried on to a very great extent. The salt taken from salt-water lakes, is piled up in vast quantities on the banks, and thence transported to different parts of the country by carriers, and, when practicable, by vessels. Its plenty and its cheapness are of great importance to the fisheries.

In the neighbourhood of the city are extensive vineyards, the site of which is generally marked by windmills, erected for the purpose of raising water for irrigation, without which assistance the parched earth would not bring the vintage to perfection. The grapes here are delicious. There are besides, a great variety of fruits; the melons are said to be the finest in the world, not excepting those of Ispahan.

The principal promenade in Astrakhan is on the banks of the canal. I was astonished to see here men and women swimming together, without the slightest regard to decency, at a time when all the principal inhabitants were taking their evening walks. This indelicate practice is very common throughout Russia. At Nishney Novogorod, I saw women walk from one bath to another, in a complete state of nudity, past a large concourse of people.

July 28.—On the 28th, Mr. Glen went with me to visit one of the sturgeon-fisheries of Mr. Ssaposhenikoff, a wealthy merchant of Astrakhan, who with the greatest civility sent us down in his own barge, having previously given orders that the fishermen should await our coming.

The distance was about thirty versts, but

we had ten active Kalmucks, who soon rowed us down. The name of this fishery is Karmaziack. The dependent village contains a population of six hundred persons. One hundred boats are employed. Two persons are in each boat; one, generally a female, rows, and the other hauls in the fish. The instruments used, are a mallet, and a stick with a large unbarbed hook at the end. Every fisherman has a certain number of lines; one line contains fifty hooks; these are placed at regular distances from each other; they are without barbs, sunk about a foot under water, and are kept in motion by small pieces of wood attached to them. The sturgeon generally swims in a large shoal near the surface. Upon being caught by one hook, he generally gets entangled with one or two more in his struggle to escape. Immediately on our arrival, the boats pushed from shore; each fisherman proceeded to take up his lines; on coming to a fish, he drew it with his hooked stick to the side of the boat, hit it a violent blow on the head with the mallet, and, after disengaging it from the other hooks, hauled it into the boat. This part of the process was excellent sport. On every side, the tremendous splashing of the water announced the capture of some huge inhabitant of the deep.

As soon as we had seen enough of this part of the business, we went into a large wooden house on the banks of the river, where a clerk was seated to take an account of the number caught. Seventy copecks is given for each fish. There were caught this morning four beloogas, one hundred and ten sturgeons, nine shevreegas, and several sterlets, a small kind of sturgeon, which, though the most delicious, are never counted. These last are distinguishable from the sturgeon by a mark above the mouth. The sterlet is almost peculiar to the Wolga, though occasionally a few are caught in the

Don. The belooga is a large fish; one of those caught to-day weighed four pood, one hundred and forty-four English pounds. The shevreega is like a pike, having a very long head. There was also a large black fish, called a som. It is very voracious, and will attack a man in the water. The head is not sold, as nobody but the Kalmucks will eat it, and they will eat any thing. It was given to our boatmen, who went off in high glee to make a meal of it.

In this house, men with instruments like boat-hooks drew the fish from the boats, and laid them in a row. Their heads were split in two; the roe, or caviar, and the isinglass were taken out and separately disposed; the bodies were cut in half and washed in a reservoir of water, thence they were taken into a large warehouse, between the walls of which are placed a quantity of ice; a few shovels of salt were thrown over them, and by this short process they became ready salted for exportation. The isinglass was taken into a room, where children were employed in laying it out either on flat boards, or rolling it up exactly in the same mode in which it is exposed for sale. The former mode constitutes what, I believe, is called the book, and the latter the sheet isinglass. In the mean time, the caviar was collected in pails, and placed on a frame of net-work over a large tub, and, by being passed to and fro, the fat fibres which connect it together were separated from it, and afterwards converted into oil. This done, thirty-five degrees of salt and water were thrown upon it, which, after being worked for twenty minutes with paddles, was drained off by a sieve, and the caviar was put into mat bags; these were squeezed well between two boards, and there the process ends. In the short space of three hours, I saw the fish caught, killed, and salted, the isinglass prepared for sale, and the salted caviar ready packed for exportation.

What we saw was the morning process. The hooks, on being separated from the fish, require no farther preparation. The fishermen go to their dinners, and in the evening make a second visit to their lines, when all the operations to which we were witnesses are repeated. In the winter, a particular spot, with deep holes, is left for a considerable time undisturbed: when the ice is sufficiently strong, the fishermen of the various fisheries assemble, and breaking holes in it throw in their nets; after two days, the pit or hole is exhausted, and scarcely one fish escapes.

Mr. Ssaposhenikoff hires these fisheries of Prince Korackchin at an annual rent of four hundred and fifty thousand roubles. Besides this fishery of Karmaziack, he has twenty-nine others: a good season will produce three hundred thousand roubles clear profit.

After having seen this interesting exhibition, we went to a small house by the waterside, where a sumptuous entertainment had been prepared for us by the polite attentions of Mr. Ssaposhenikoff. We had a great variety of wines; but that which deserves particular notice, was a bottle of London porter, which had arrived at this remote and inland quarter in a state of perfect preservation.

As I was stepping into the boat, the superintendent of the fisheries presented me with some book-isinglass, and a bag of salted caviar from the fish which I had seen alive four hours before.

CHAPTER X.

Departure from Astrakhan—Mode of dispersing Locusts—Colony of Sarepta—Modern Hippophagi—German Colonies—Russian travelling—Saratoff—Penza—Nishney Novogorod—Effect of an Uniform—A Cossack Sentry—Rascolnicks—Horsemanship—Theatre—Russian dance.

On the 30th of July I quitted the hospitable roof of Mr. Glen, and resumed my journey, for the purpose of being present at the grand annual fair which is held at Nishney Novogorod. I was accompanied from Astrakhan by Mr. James Mitchell, a young man, the son of a Missionary, whose father paid me the compliment to commit him to my care. Mr. Mitchell, who is a native of the colony of Karass, had never been farther north than Astrakhan. He travelled with me as far as St. Petersburgh, and proved of the greatest service to me; as, besides Oriental languages, he was well acquainted with Russian and German: so we managed very well on the road, being able between us to speak eight different languages.

We were escorted to the opposite bank of the Wolga by all the English residents of the city, who came to bid farewell to their young friend. Our carriage hence was a kibitka, which had been given us by the Missionaries.

For the first time during my long journey I was this evening caught in a shower of rain. We traversed the grand steppe or desert of Astrakhan for two days. On the evening of the 1st of August we arrived at a Russian village, which was surrounded by a considerable tract of well-cultivated land. While changing horses, I witnessed what was to me a very curious sight: a vast flight of locusts, extending fifteen miles, suddenly made their appearance from the east, and came in a huge phalanx to attack the crops. In an instant every villager was on the road to his own field. Some took dogs, others were on horseback, and others ran shouting and clapping their hands all the way, the inhabitants finding from experience that the locusts very much dislike noise. My fellow-traveller told me, that in the colony of Karass, when the locusts come in sight, not only all the inhabitants, but the military, turn out, and endeavour to drive them off by drums and fifes, and a perpetual discharge of musketry. The enemy thus repulsed make a speedy retreat, and commit their depredations on the lands of those who are less on the alert to resist them.

August 3.—It is difficult to describe the pleasurable sensations with which I entered the beautiful little town of Sarepta, after having been for four days and nights travelling through an almost barren waste. There had been no previous indication to point out the haunts of man, when Sarepta, seated in the bosom of a rich valley, suddenly burst on the view. Our carriage passed through small but regular streets, and stopped at the door of the inn, a neat house, in a pretty square, which, together with the church at the opposite end, brought the snug villages of England to my mind. We were here received by a respectable-looking old German, who soon laid before us a dinner, that did not destroy the illusion of home in which I had indulged.

The greater part of Sarepta was destroyed by fire two years ago; but the active little colony is fast repairing the devastation, and new buildings are rearing their heads in every direction. It is gratifying to know, that the principal funds which enabled them to rebuild the town, are derived from a London subscription.

In the morning we were waited upon by a deputation of the inhabitants, begging us to visit their shops. Every member of this infant republic being anxious to exert his interests for the general good, our landlord was particularly solicitous in seconding this request. His motive for so doing is gratitude for a law of the colony in his favour, which prevents any one of their number from asking a stranger to dinner, as such invitation would be prejudicial to his interest as an innkeeper and a member of the commonwealth. In return for this excellent decree, he puffs off the goods of his fellow-citizens to every new comer, which obliges them, as it did me, to purchase some trifle at every house. As for myself, I returned home laden with gingerbread and baby-linen, and tobacco. I afterwards went to visit a Moravian establishment. Opposite the inn formerly stood a house containing eighty bachelors, and near it one containing eighty spinsters. The house of the former has been burnt down; that of the latter has escaped. The females divide their own dwelling with the men till theirs is rebuilt. When a bachelor is tired of a life of celibacy, he goes next door, chooses one out of the eighty spinsters, and makes her his wife. The pair become members of the general community, and keep house for themselves. The vacancies are filled up by the children of those who had once been inmates of these mansions of single blessedness.

I was highly gratified with my visit to this human hive. Every thing was in the neatest order; the sisters, as they are called, with their little caps and uniform dress, reminded me of our fair Quakers. The female children were reading and writing; the young women were engaged in domestic employments. The old maids, for there were a few, were occupied in knitting and needlework. All were busy at the occupation best adapted to their peculiar habits and talents. Nor were the brothers idle; here were shoemakers, tailors, weavers, printers, and bookbinders. I was shown a fine collection of the serpents and other reptiles of Southern Russia. I saw also a large collection of antiquities found in the neighbourhood, which proves the former existence of an ancient city on this spot.

I regret that the anxiety to pursue my journey prevented my giving the necessary time to these relics; but I was obliged, though with regret, to take a hasty leave of the Sarepta community.

Before we bade farewell to our Moravian friends, we visited their burying-ground. Even this partakes of republican simplicity.

It is a square enclosure. The tombstones are exactly alike, being three feet by two. On each is inscribed, without comment, the Christian and surname of the deceased, and the day on which he died. These humble testimonials of the dead are singularly contrasted with the aristocratic marble tombstone of a Russian Princess who is buried here.

We left Sarepta at three in the afternoon. Eight miles west of the town is a mineral spring: near it are a suite of baths. The inhabitants of Sarepta bathe here once a week: in the month of May, people come from a distance to take the benefit of its medicinal effects.

August 4.—We travelled all night, and at daylight reached a village, where we changed horses. One of the poor beasts died as he was taken from off the carriage: some Kalmucks immediately carried him away for their breakfast. Ptolemy designates a tribe of Scythians (Tartars) by the name of Ἱπ-ποφαγι, or Horse-eaters.

August 5.—On the morning of the 5th, we fell in with some German colonies, which occupy a tract of land extending hence to the north of Saratoff. It was not till we arrived among these settlers that we saw any thing like regular cultivation: corn is very abundant here: each driver seated himself on a bag of flour, with which he fed his cattle at the end of the stage. In the desert we had just quitted, wormwood is the principal, and sometimes the only food for the horse. We passed through several German villages, and were struck with the appearance of the broad hats of the women. Vast quantities of buck-wheat are grown here: the lower orders make it up into a porridge, of which they are very fond.

I cannot agree with those who speak in favour of Russian travelling. Its only merit is its extreme cheapness. Sometimes our road was formed of the trunks of trees: on these occasions, off would go our driver at full gallop; and as we passed over holes made by the fracture of timber, the kibitka would spring into the air, and return with such a bound that I often expected dislocation of a bone must follow. It is true, this painful ordeal may be alleviated by having springs to the carriage; but the remedy is worse than the disorder. Few springs can stand such a violent shock; and if they are once broken, there will be great difficulty in having them repaired.

The traveller is recommended to be careful in having old instead of new wheels to his carriage. Those of ours were new; the consequence of which was, in a short time they were so warped by the sun, that one or two spokes fell out every day, till at last only four remained in one of the fellies. By great good luck I succeeded in purchasing another set of wheels, for which I willingly gave five times their value.

Another grievance on a Russian journey is the vexatious delay the traveller undergoes from the conduct of the smatreetels or superintendents of the post-houses, who will refuse horses to any one weak enough to submit to such treatment. With Mr. Mitchell for interpreter, I occasionally addressed these men in rather strong language. One of them, from whom I had, by dint of abuse and threats, succeeded in obtaining a relay of cattle, vented his spleen on my fellow-traveller; saying, that he should report his conduct for having spoken disrespectfully to one of his rank. My young friend, who, though not a soldier himself, had been bred up in all due veneration for military precedence, seemed alarmed at the consequences of having wounded the dignity of a smatreetel, who, he assured me, ranked as "an officer of the fourteenth class." When angry words failed, I used to bribe these "officers" with twopence, an affront their dignity generally pocketed with a bow. I know but of one more mode for insuring the good offices of the smatreetel, which I shall illustrate in an anecdote of a French nobleman:—This personage, an *attaché* to the embassy, being on his journey from St. Petersburgh to Moscow, had been, as usual, delayed on the road for want of horses, the smatreetel telling him that there were none in the stable. He had one day been deploring his hard fate a full hour, when a Cossack officer with despatches arrived at the post-house. To dismount from his *arba*, to unsling his whip from his own shoulder, to lay it across that of the smatreetel, to have fresh horses attached to his vehicle, and to be again on his journey, was but the work of a moment. The hint was not thrown away on the Frenchman: he immediately unlocked his portmanteau, took out his Parisian cane, and imitated the action of the Cossack. The effect was equally instantaneous. The little cane, like the wand of Cinderella's fairy godmother, was no sooner waved, than a coach and horses appeared, and carried off the French magician, who, by repeating the secret of his newly acquired art, reached Moscow a day sooner than he had any reason to expect.

August 7.—At Saratoff, the capital of the district so called, we found the houses had all been lately whitewashed, and the streets put in repair, in expectation of the Emperor Alexander's arrival. As we proceeded, we found the verst-posts and bridges newly painted, and the road patched up and sanded for the same occasion. We were, however, not allowed to profit by these improvements. The repairs were of such a nature, as to be only just sufficient to sustain the weight of the imperial retinue; so we poor travellers were doomed, by an ukase, to jog on by the road side, to have ease and luxury in sight, but to have them denied to every sense.

August 8.—We reached Penza, another capital town, in the afternoon of the 8th. Every body was in the bustle of preparation; a large body of troops were assembled for the purpose of being reviewed by the Emperor. The same active preparations were going on as at Saratoff, and the vamping system was in still greater force. Bricklayers and plasterers were fully occupied. Opposite the place where we changed horses, they were literally pulling down an old house, as too unseemly an object for autocratic eyes. The town was crowded with military. Generals, attended by their aides-de-camp and orderlies, were seen prancing through the streets. Large smoking groups of wasp-waisted huzzars met the eye at every turn. Every thing partook of "the pomp and circumstance of glorious war." A crowd is always to me a gratifying sight; it was doubly so on arriving from a thinly-populated country. The review was expected to take place very shortly: with any other place but home for my destination, I would gladly have stayed to witness the Russian system of evolutions.

August 9.—We arrived at Nishney Novogorod on the 9th, at the height of the grand annual fair, hired lodgings, and then sallied forth into the crowd in search of amusement. But my ideas had been so associated with the boyish recollections of Gooseberry-fair,* and its numerous wild-beasts, booths, swings, and merry-go-rounds, that I was wofully disappointed in witnessing the noiseless, orderly, and stupid scene at Nishney Novogorod. Here were no national

* In my time, Gooseberry-fair was held every Easter and Whitsuntide, in the Westminsters' cricket-ground of Tothill-fields. The field is now enclosed, and subsequent improvements have destroyed all the enjoyments of that dirty, yet delightful quarter.

pastimes, not even a *Montagne Russe.*— Though merchants had assembled from every quarter of the globe, they had come on business, not pleasure. The few Russian noblemen present had estates in the neighbourhood, and had come to collect their rents. Indeed, I question whether, out of this vast concourse, I was not the only person who had been attracted hither solely by motives of curiosity and amusement. Still, to a person who has always lived in a crowd, this motley assemblage could not be without its interest; and before I left Neshney Novogorod, I managed to extract more amusement than I had expected.

The place in which the fair is held is encircled by a canal of an oblong form. Within this space are several formal lines of roofed shops or warehouses, in which articles are exposed for sale, without any attention to the attractive order of their arrangement. British goods seemed to be in high repute;

and often, in passing along a row of shops, did I hear the venders of some flimsy articles puffing them off as being "Anglicansky"—English.

For the first day I was dressed in a plain blue coat, and wandered through the fair friendless and forlorn; Mr. Mitchell being unable to render me assistance as an interpreter, from the diffidence he naturally felt at having thus suddenly fallen in with so great a concourse of people. Tired of this neglect, I next morning, by the advice of my fellow-traveller, tried the effect of a military dress. Not the disguised corsair in Sheridan's "Critic," when he first discovers his embroidered waistcoat, could have produced a greater change on his beholders, than did I on mine in my aide-de-camp's uniform. Those who had jostled me the day before, now vied with each other in paying me attention: the Director of the fair solicited the honour of being my cicerone; and I, who in the morning could not boast of an acquaintance, found myself in the evening possessed of fifty friends.

In the course of the day, I paid my respects to General Groukoff, the Governor. He received me very civilly, and begged I would make his house my home during my stay. I dined with him this afternoon; and in the evening met at his house the Prince of Georgia, and several other Russian noblemen.

As it rained hard when I was about to return home, I borrowed an old hat and coat from one of my fifty friends, to save my military dress. In following the banks of the canal to arrive at the bridge, I felt myself suddenly arrested by the muscular grasp of a man, whom I discovered to be a huge Cossack on sentry. With a broad grin on his savage features, he grasped his horrible whip, and, beckoning a comrade, motioned by signs too plain to be misunderstood, what would be the alternative if I did not give him money for something to drink. With all a Westminster's science in boxing, it would have been in vain to have contended with two armed men, so I gave him a small silver coin; but as this did not satisfy him, he had already raised his arm for punishment, when I opened my coat and showed my military boots and spurs, and, with all the Russian I was master of, told him that I was an English officer and an acquaintance of the Governor's.

It was evident I had made myself perfectly understood, for he quitted his hold as though I had been a serpent, relaxed his grin, and took with him his comrade, who had just arrived to assist him in his depredation. Upon enquiry, I heard that such a line of conduct was very common with these ruffians, who not unfrequently rob and murder merchants falling within their grasp. The next morning I reported the circumstance to the Governor, and am inclined to believe the Cossack underwent the punishment he had designed for me.

August 11.—As I was looking at a collection of Siberian minerals, which were enclosed in a glass case, I observed an old man with a long beard similarly engaged. On his entering the room, I was struck with the marked coldness shown him by every one present : by chance, his elbow broke one of the glasses : the company seemed delighted at his having accidentally furnished them with a grievance : they simultaneously left the room, and returned with a corporal and file of the guard, to whom they gave him in charge. On enquiring, in a tone of pity, the reason for this hard usage, I was answered that he was a “ Rascolnick,” a dissenter from the Greek church ; and therefore, said my informer, unworthy of your sympathy.

There are many dissenters under the general term of Rascolnick : one of these sects, chiefly in the south of Russia, become eunuchs. The Emperor Alexander tried to put them down, but without success.

I accompanied the Director this afternoon to see some feats of horsemanship. The performer, who was a Frenchman, danced on the bare back of a horse with considerable skill; but, as I could see this sort of sight at home, I turned my attention to one much more interesting—the spectators. Assembled round the equestrian ring were natives of nearly every country of Asia, all dressed in their national garb, and exhibiting features as varied as their dresses. I was particularly attracted by the wonder expressed by some Tartar horse-catchers, who, great equestrians themselves, knew not what to make of this kind of riding. "Look! look!" said the Director, pointing to the rider; but I was too busy in watching the variety of animated nature to waste a moment on the performances of art.

From the Circus we went to the Theatre.

The performance was Kotzebue's play of "Pizarro, or The Death of Rolla," as it is here called. The acting was respectable, and the play differed but little from Sheridan's translation. Rolla was in the hands of a young man whose violent declamations in favour of liberty induced me to ask who he was. I was informed that he and the rest of the troop were "the slaves" of a neighbouring prince, who had let them out at so much a-head to a strolling Impresario!

The amusements closed with the national Russian dance. It was very entertaining; and, like most exhibitions of this nature, described the usual process of a courtship;—a proper degree of importunity on the one hand, resistance and ultimate consent on the other. The female dancer here, a pretty lively coquette, suddenly attracted by my scarlet coat, transferred her attentions from her partner on the stage to me in the pit, to the no small amusement of the spectators, myself not excepted.

CHAPTER XI.

Arrival at Moscow—Messrs. Hart and Lamb—Governor General — Military Honours — Gallitsin Hospital — Burning of Moscow—The Kremlin—The Diligence—State Prisoner—Arrival in England.

August 12. — Mr. Mitchell and I left Nishney Novogorod on the evening of the 12th, and travelled night and day till we reached Moscow, a distance of four hundred and forty-three versts, on the morning of the 15th.

August 15.—It is hardly possible to imagine any thing more beautiful than the first appearance of this city, combining, as it does, the architecture of almost every age and every country: the gilded dome of the Mahometan era in Asia, the Gothic walls and towers of the rude ages of Europe, and the Grecian structures of a more cultivated period.

I had not been long settled in my hotel, when I heard that two English travellers had just arrived from Persia. I immediately sent my name to them, and soon after in walked Messrs. Hart and Lamb, by whom, it will be remembered, I had sent letters for my family from Tabriz, in the expectation that they would have arrived in England six weeks before me. We were all mutually gratified at this rencontre, and agreed not to separate again until we should reach home.

August 17.—This morning we paid our respects to Prince Demetrio Gallitsin, the Governor-General of Moscow. Captain Hart wore the uniform of the 4th Light Dragoons, and I that of an aide-de-camp. As both our dresses were similar to those worn by Russian general officers, all the guards of the city turned out, and received us with military honours. In the anti-room of the Governor-General, I saw the Commander of the forces, informed him of our having received such unmerited compliments, and begged, that to prevent a recurrence of them, he would be good enough to explain to the guards our actual rank in the army. He answered with much politeness, that no attentions were too great for English gentlemen, who were pleased to honour his country with a visit; and that so far from giving directions to the guards to discontinue the compliment, he should be much displeased if they did not always pay those distinctions which he considered our due.

When we came in, there were several officers of high rank waiting for an audience; but the moment we were announced, the Governor-General desired that we might be admitted. His Excellency is a highly polished and agreeable man. He behaved to us with the greatest affability, and kept us in conversation for a considerable time. He asked us several questions relative to our numerical force in India, and our expedition against the Burmese, of which he seemed to have received very recent accounts. As there was no idea of a war when we left Bombay, and as we had had no means of gaining intelligence during our journey, we treated the matter very lightly, assuring him that Burmah would never dare to make a stand against us. His Excellency looked incredulous at this observation, evidently attributing to deep diplomacy, what was, in fact, mere ignorance.

We returned in the evening to dine with his Excellency; a large company was assembled to meet his Royal Highness the

Duke of Wurtemburg. Before we could make our bows to the Governor-General, we had to force our way through crowds of star-adorned nobility, to many of whom we were presented.

His Excellency behaved to us with the most marked attention. At dinner, he placed me opposite him, and desired two noblemen, who had been in England, to sit on each side of me. In compliment to us, his Excellency spoke nothing but English during the repast, and whenever he was not occupied in attentions to his royal guest, he addressed himself entirely to my fellow-travellers and myself.

On Sunday we attended divine service at the Gallitsin Hospital, a charitable institution founded in 1802 by Prince Gallitsin. The Chapel is an elegant building, surmounted by a dome. The service was very impressively performed, and there was a great appearance of devotion in the congregation, many of whom frequently threw themselves on their faces in the Oriental manner. The singing, the only music allowed in Greek churches, was the most melodious I ever heard. The priest chanted in a loud sonorous tone, and the responses were made by a choir of concealed singers, whose voices were so delightfully harmonized, that I had difficulty in persuading myself they were not the notes of an organ. Scott mentions, in one of his novels,* the effect on the senses of music, when the performers are concealed; and I was struck this morning with the truth of the observation.

During our stay at Moscow, we heard various versions of the burning of Moscow in 1812. We were told that Count Rastopchin, at that time Governor-General of Moscow, had published three separate accounts: one for the Russians, attributing the burning to the French; a second for the English,

* Bride of Lammermoor.

avowing the burning himself; and a third for the French, leaving it in doubt who was the incendiary. He was in disgrace when we were here, and we did not see him. My old friend and school-fellow Mr. Carr Glyn speaks of him as an amiable, agreeable, and clever person, and thinks with myself that his character has been much abused. Rastopchin burnt his own country-house before the entry of the French into Moscow. The Russian army is said to have been drunk at the time, and to have pillaged the city to a great extent. The Muscovites tell you, that if Napoleon, after the battle of Smolensko, had taken up his quarters in Poland, had given the Poles a free constitution, and had freed the peasants in Russia and the Tartars in the Crimea, success would have attended him the following year.

On our arrival here, orders had been issued to close the Palace of the Kremlin, for the purpose of making some repairs; but the

Governor-General, hearing us express a wish to visit it, with the greatest politeness sent to suspend the projected operations till after we had seen the curiosities. We were met at the door of the palace by a general officer, who very civilly pointed out to us every thing worthy of interest.

The jewel-chamber contains a number of gold and silver vases, goblets, and other vessels, of which I have neither time nor inclination to make particular mention. Round the walls are the thrones of different monarchs, and standing on separate pedestals are numerous crowns, including those of Kazan, Astrakhan, Siberia, Georgia, and Poland, the sight of which brought to mind the gradual increase of this vast empire. We were shown the large boots of Peter the Great, and the coronation coat of the Emperor Alexander. This last is of a green colour, perfectly plain, and the cloth of as coarse a texture as that worn by sergeants of our army.

A public diligence is established between the two capitals, and leaves Moscow every Tuesday, Friday, and Saturday morning at nine o'clock. It stops each day half an hour for breakfast, and an hour for dinner or supper. The traveller is allowed twenty pounds' weight of luggage, and pays twenty copecks for every pound above that weight. The inside places are one hundred and twenty roubles, and those in the cabriolet sixty. In winter the charges are considerably less.

As our party amounted to four, we engaged a diligence for our private accommodation, and agreed to leave Moscow on the Wednesday; but an ague, an old Indian acquaintance, having paid me a visit, our departure was protracted. By the rules of the post, if travellers are unable to proceed the day on which they have engaged the diligence, they forfeit their places; but as another instance of the Governor General's attention, he desired that the diligence should wait our convenience. Luckily for the party, I was sufficiently well to commence the journey the following afternoon.

A man with a tertian ague upon him is not a likely person to appreciate the charms of any journey, still less of such a fatiguing one as that from Moscow to Saint Petersburgh.

One morning, as we were changing horses, a state prisoner, guarded and heavily manacled, drove up to the inn door. He looked pale and dispirited; no one appeared to be acquainted with the nature of his accusation. He had been suddenly taken from his family at Vladimir, had been travelling night and day, and was not to be allowed to stop till he arrived at St. Petersburgh. It was with a shudder I heard that he was, in all probability, likely to perish under the dreadful lash of the knout.

From Novogorod to St. Petersburgh, the last forty versts of the journey, we travelled over a macadamized road. After a detention of three weeks at the Russian capital, we sailed for England. At the dawn of a dull, misty, but to me delightful morning of November, we made the Suffolk coast; nearly at the same moment we hailed a herring-smack, which landed me at Lowestoft, thirty-five miles from my own home, and I had the gratification of dining with my family the same evening.

THE END.

INDEX.

A.

B.

D.

E.

F.

G.

H.

I.

J.

K.

L.

M.

N.

R.

S.

T.

X.

Y.

Z.